George Washington's
False Teeth

NEW YORK

LONDON

GEORGE
WASHINGTON'S
FALSE TEETH

ROBERT DARNTON

W · W · NORTON & COMPANY

An

Unconventional

Guide

to the

Eighteenth

Century

Page 1 (page x, detail): *George Washington at Princeton*, by Charles Willson Peale, 1779, oil on canvas, 93 × 58.5 in. (236.2 × 148.6 cm.), Acc. no. 1943.16.2. Courtesy of the Pennsylvania Academy of the Fine Arts, Philadelphia. Gift of Maria McKean Allen and Phebe Warren Downes through the bequest of their mother, Elizabeth Wharton McKean.

For information about permission to reproduce selections from this book, write to Permissions, W. W. Norton & Company, Inc., 500 Fifth Avenue, New York, NY 10110

Manufacturing by The Haddon Craftsmen, Inc.
Book design by Margaret M. Wagner
Production manager: Amanda Morrison

Library of Congress Cataloging-in-Publication Data

Darnton, Robert.
George Washington's false teeth : an unconventional guide to the eighteenth century / Robert Darnton
p. cm.
Includes bibliographical references and index.
ISBN 0-393-05760-7
1. France—Intellectual life—18th century. 2. Enlightenment—France. I. Title.

DC33.4.D36 2003

2002044481

W. W. Norton & Company, Inc.
500 Fifth Avenue, New York, N.Y. 10110
www.wwnorton.com

W. W. Norton & Company Ltd.
Castle House, 75/76 Wells Street, London W1T 3QT

1 2 3 4 5 6 7 8 9 0

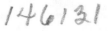

CONTENTS

INTRODUCTION

THE FATHER OF HIS COUNTRY FIGHTING TOOTHACHE? It was not the least of his battles, and he finally lost it. Having defeated the British and won the first election to the presidency, he was inaugurated in 1789 with one tooth in his mouth, a lower left bicuspid. If you know how to look, you can see the effects of his losses on the dental front by inspecting his portraits—not the Gilbert Stuart on the dollar bill, or the famous Stuart of 1796 in which the artist packed cotton behind Washington's lips to make them look more natural, but the portrait of 1779 by Charles Willson Peale (see Figure 1), which shows the scar on the caved-in area beneath his left cheekbone, the result, it seems, of a fistula from an abscessed tooth. Washington was worked over by all the best-known dentists of the country. He had a large collection of false teeth, made of everything from elephant ivory, walrus tusk, and hippopotamus tusk to the teeth of a fellow human.[1] Nor was he alone in his war against tooth disease. His contemporaries probably worried more about the pain in their gums than about the new constitution in 1787. But they were an odd lot, if seen up close.

In fact, everything about the eighteenth century is strange, once you examine it in detail. The carriage of the marquis de Sade gets stuck in a traffic jam, and in a fit of road rage he runs his sword

Fig. 1. *George Washington at Princeton*, 1779, detail. Gift of the Executors of the Elizabeth Wharton McKean Estate, 1943.16.2. Courtesy of the Pennsylvania Academy of the Fine Arts.

through a horse's belly. The chevalier d'Eon announces he is a woman and stages dueling matches in drag. Lafayette decorates his Paris town house with American Indians in native costume, while Marie-Antoinette dresses up as a milkmaid and manufactures a village in the gardens of Versailles. The eighteenth century is always adopting disguises and changing costumes.

It is also full of civic lessons. It makes declarations—of independence in America, of the rights of man in France—and it publishes treatises: *The Spirit of the Laws*, *The Social Contract*. But it adds strange twists to its apologies for liberty. Montesquieu takes cues from Machiavelli and imagines a revolution erupting from a harem. Rousseau draws on Hobbes in an attempt to bind democracy to the General Will. And Mirabeau invokes Rousseau in order to manipulate the Bourse. Visit the eighteenth century, and you will return with your head spinning, for it is endlessly surprising, inexhaustibly interesting, irresistibly strange.

The taste for strangeness does not suit the favorite flavors of history in the United States, but it could produce some positive effects, if only as an antidote to false historical consciousness. When the country faces catastrophe, Americans often turn to the Founding Fathers for help, as though we could open a direct line to the eighteenth century and tap a font of wisdom. During the debates about impeaching Presidents Nixon and Clinton, for example, we tried to find a way out of the crises by poring over every scrap of paper produced by the men who had sat in the Constitutional Convention. Yet they lived in a different world from ours. Open the correspondence between Jefferson and Madison, and you will stumble upon remarks like the following: "The earth belongs always to the living generation. . . . Every constitution then, and every law, naturally expires [sic] at the end of 19 years. If it be enforced longer, it is an act of force, and not of right."[2] If we venture far enough into "the lost world of Thomas Jefferson," as Daniel Boorstin called it, we are likely to get lost ourselves.

This book provides a guide to the eighteenth century, not to all of it (that would require a multivolume treatise) but to some of its most curious, out-of-the-way corners and also to its main concern, the cause of the Enlightenment. I first imagined writing such a guidebook long ago while attempting to follow Jefferson through Paris. His trail led into the lives of Frenchmen who mixed an idealistic passion for America with bareknuckled politics in Grub Street. One of them, Étienne Clavière, actually got caught in a punch-up on the Paris Bourse, and his speculations involved him simultaneously in projects to found a utopian colony in Ohio and in plots to bring down the government in Versailles. Another Americophile, Jacques-Pierre Brissot, turned up as a spy in the archives of the lieutenant general of police. The lines of inquiry opened onto so much unfamiliar territory that I finally decided to follow them instead of Jefferson and spent the next decades roaming around in the field of study known in France as the history of mentalities. The essays brought together here are field reports on that experience. But they do not wander all over the eighteenth-century map. They concentrate on four interrelated themes: French-American connections, life in the Republic of Letters, modes of communication, and ways of thought peculiar to the French Enlightenment.

Each of these themes offers a way into the remote mental world of the eighteenth century, but each also has some affinity with contemporary issues, and that poses a problem. "Thou shalt not commit anachronism" is the historian's first commandment. We may break it if we draw connections between the present and the past. The danger of "presentism," as it is sometimes called, is more insidious than it seems. Few historians sift through the past for moral lessons or imagine Washington as one of us, dressed up in period costume. But how can we see him except through our own eyes, looking back through our own time? Is there not a presentist bias built into the frame of our perception? And how can we get a direct view of him even when we contemplate the paintings of Gilbert Stuart and Charles Willson Peale? There is no unmediated access to the past.

Historians deal with this dilemma by embracing a professional ethos. They try to reconstruct the past "as it actually was," according to standards set by Ranke following Thucydides.[3] But this commitment comes at a cost, for professional history tends to be esoteric, and professional historians often write for one another, cut off from the general public by a protective wall of erudition. This book is intended to break through that barrier. It is written for the general educated reader and is meant to provide historical perspective to current questions such as: Does the adoption of the euro challenge notions about the identity of Europe? Has the Internet created a new information society? Can the obsession with the private lives of public figures expose fault lines in political culture? By projecting those questions against an eighteenth-century background, I think it is possible to see them in a new light, while at the same time enjoying a fresh view of the eighteenth century.

That may sound like unashamed anachronism. I hope, however, to cope with the presentist element implicit in any picture of the past by acknowledging it and putting it up front. My argument is not that the eighteenth century was strange in itself—Washington did not think it odd to be deprived of twenty-first-century dentistry—but rather that it is strange to us. By confronting that strangeness, we can get to know it better. We also may be able to fight off a threat that comes from the opposite extreme, what the French call *passéisme*. An obsession with the past may distort it by magnifying everything that makes it peculiar and by blowing its peculiarities out of proportion. This sin goes under a different name among anthropologists: othering. For several years now they have issued warnings against attributing too much otherness to other cultures. To insist on the exotic uniqueness of another people may be to get them wrong in a way that puts them out of reach.[4] Similarly, to make the past appear as too remote a foreign land may be to cut off access to it. Instead of reifying foreign cultures in the hope of capturing something imagined as their essence, we need to interrogate them. We need to learn to speak their languages, to put the right questions to the relevant sources, and to translate the answers back into an idiom that can be understood by our contemporaries.

If you put that program into practice, you cannot avoid a confrontation with your own subjectivity. History, like anthropology, has shifted to a self-reflective mode, but it need not succumb to egocentricity any more than to ethnocentricity, as I hope these essays show. Some of them are written in the first person singular, which used to be taboo among professionals who tried to create an illusion of objectivity by maintaining a proper rhetorical distance between their subjects and themselves. Rather than deny subjectivity, I am trying in this book to honor a second commandment, "Thou shalt not other," even though it cuts against the first. I see no easy way around the double danger of *passéisme* and presentism, except to shuttle back and forth across the centuries, looking for fresh perspectives. But that, as I understand it, is the value of history: not to teach lessons but to provide perspective.

It also gives pleasure, especially for those who commute to the eighteenth century. The age of the Founding Fathers had serious business before it, but it also had fun. It cocked snooks, cut rugs, lowered booms, and pursued happiness of every variety. Unfortunately, however, it also had bad teeth. Anyone who roams around in the eighteenth century keeps coming up against toothache. The most famous character in eighteenth-century Paris, aside from the public hangman, was Le Grand Thomas, a tooth puller who operated on the Pont-Neuf and cut quite a figure according to a contemporary description of him:

> He could be recognized from a great distance by his gigantic size and the amplitude of his clothing. Mounted on a steel cart, his head held high and covered in brilliant plumes, he . . . made his virile voice boom out to both ends of the bridge and both sides of the Seine. He was surrounded by a trusting public; toothaches seemed to expire at his feet. His zealous admirers, like an inexhaustible flood, crowded around him and never took their eyes off him. Hands lifted in the air, imploring his remedies, and doctors could be seen scuttling away along the sidewalk, raging inwardly with jealousy at his success.[5]

Most of us today don't bother much about our teeth, except for the occasional quick fix at our dentist. If we listened to the eighteenth century, we would hear humanity grinding its teeth, such as they were, in a constant struggle against pain. Not even the king was immune. The doctors of Louis XIV broke his jaw trying to extract rotten molars. And the cult of Washington owes a good deal to his dentures. My own dentist assures me that the false teeth of the Founding Father show up everywhere in dentistry textbooks and that jokes about them are standard fare in dental schools. For example:

Dental student A: Why does George Washington look so pained on the dollar bill?

Dental student B: Wooden dentures.

Dental student A: No, it's because he didn't make it to the twenty-dollar bill.

Did Washington really wear false teeth made of wood? I thought I saw them long ago at Mount Vernon, but Mount Vernon now has a Web page, which warns that the wooden teeth are a myth. Perhaps I should have extracted them from chapter 1—and also from chapter 4, where they briefly reappear—but I have left them there nonetheless, because they belong to the mythical dimension of history, which is another subject of this book. Myths shaped mentalities, and they too can be found in strange places, like eighteenth-century salons, where they provided Condorcet with material for imagining himself as a *bourgeois de New Haven* and Brissot with an opportunity to pursue exotic Americans in Paris—not just Lafayette and his Indians but Hector Saint John de Crèvecoeur, the Norman turned American farmer who passed as an expert on noble savages.

The Web itself is surrounded by a myth, the notion that it ushered in a new phase of history, "the information age." In this respect as well, the eighteenth century offers an opportunity for us to sharpen our historical consciousness, for it too was an age of information with media of its own, and they transmitted messages that can still be picked up from the surviving documentation. On a good day in the archives, one can even piece together parts of the communication system through which they flowed. That historical task coincides with the general goal of this book: to open up lines of communication with the eighteenth century and, by following them to their sources, to understand the century "as it actually was," in all its strangeness.

1

THE CASE FOR THE ENLIGHTENMENT: GEORGE WASHINGTON'S FALSE TEETH

WE LIVE IN AN AGE OF INFLATION: INFLATED MONEY, INFLATED GRADES, INFLATED LETTERS OF RECOMMENDATION, INFLATED REPUTATIONS, AND INFLATED IDEAS. The general puffery has affected our understanding of the movement at the beginning of modern political culture, the eighteenth-century Enlightenment, because it too has been blown up to such a size that it would not be recognized by the men who first created it. Having been floated at first with a few *bons mots* in some Parisian salons, it became a campaign to crush *l'infâme,* a march of progress, a spirit of the age, a secular faith, a world view to be defended or combated or transcended, and the source of everything good, bad, and modern, including liberalism, capitalism, imperialism, male chauvinism, world federalism, UNESCO humanism, and the Family of Man. Whoever has a bone to pick or a cause to defend begins with the Enlightenment.

We scholars have added to the confusion because we have created a huge industry, Enlightenment Studies, with its own associations, journals, monograph series, congresses, and foundations. Like all professionals, we keep expanding our territory. At last count, there were thirty professional societies on six of the seven continents (Antarctica is still resisting), and at our last world congresses we listened to papers on the Russian Enlightenment, the Romanian Enlightenment, the Brazilian Enlightenment, the Josephinian Enlightenment, the Pietistic Enlightenment, the Jewish Enlightenment, the musical Enlightenment, the religious Enlightenment, the radical Enlightenment, the conservative Enlightenment, and the Confucian Enlightenment. The Enlightenment is beginning to be everything and therefore nothing.

I

I propose deflation. Let us consider the Enlightenment as a movement, a cause, a campaign to change minds and reform institutions. Like all movements, it had a beginning, a middle, and, in some places but not others, an end. It was a concrete historical phenomenon, which can be located in time and pinned down in space: Paris in the early eighteenth century. Of course it had origins. What movement does not? They extended back to antiquity and covered the map of Europe. Cartesian doubt, Newtonian physics, Lockean epistemology, the cosmologies of Leibniz and Spinoza, the natural law of Grotius and Pufendorf, the skepticism of Bayle, the biblical criticism of Richard Simon, the toleration of the Dutch, the Pietism of the Germans, the political theories and freethinking of the English: One could list philosophical sources at length, and many historians have done so. But to compile the sources is to miss the point, for the Enlightenment was less than the sum of its philosophical parts, and few of the *philosophes* were original philosophers.

They were men of letters. Only rarely did they develop ideas undreamed of in earlier generations. Compare Voltaire with Pascal, Condillac with Locke, Diderot with Descartes, Laplace with Newton, d'Holbach with Leibniz. The *philosophes* worked variations on themes set for them by their predecessors. Nature, reason, toleration, happiness, skepticism, individualism, civil liberty, cosmopolitanism: All can be found, at greater depth, in the thought of the seventeenth century. They can be found among eighteenth-century thinkers unconnected or opposed to the *philosophes*, such as Vico, Haller, Burke, and Samuel Johnson. What, then, set the *philosophes* apart?

Commitment to a cause. *Engagement.* The *philosophe* was a new social type, known to us today as the intellectual. He meant to put his ideas to use, to persuade, propagandize, and change the world around him. To be sure, earlier thinkers had also hoped to modify the world. The religious radicals and the humanists of the sixteenth century were devoted to their causes. But the *philosophes* represented a new force in history, men of letters acting in concert and with considerable autonomy to push through a program. They developed a collective identity, forged by common commitment in the face of common risks. They were marked as a group by persecution, just enough to dramatize their daring and not enough to deter them from undertaking more. They developed a strong sense of "us" against "them": men of wit against the bigots, *honnêtes hommes* against exclusive privilege, the children of light against the demons of darkness.

They were also an elite. Despite the leveling tendency inherent in their faith in reason, they aimed to take over the commanding heights of culture and to enlighten from above. This strategy led them to concentrate on the conquest of salons and academies, journals and theaters, Masonic lodges and key cafés, where they could win the rich and powerful to their cause and even gain access, by back doors and boudoirs, to the throne. They reached a broad public among the middle classes, but they drew a line above the peasantry. Better not teach peasants how to read, said Voltaire; someone had to plow the fields.

This view, I realize, is heresy. It is politically incorrect. Although it allows for the influence of royal mistresses and *grandes dames* in the salons, it concentrates on men. It is elitist, Voltairean, and incorrigibly Parisian. What about the famous cosmopolitanism of the Enlightenment? And the great thinkers not merely outside Paris but beyond the boundaries of France? Although I consider Paris the capital of the Republic of Letters in the eighteenth century, I agree that the Enlightenment spread from many sites: Edinburgh, Naples, Halle, Amsterdam, Geneva, Berlin, Milan, Lisbon, London, and even Philadelphia. Each city had its philosophers, many of whom corresponded with the *philosophes*, and quite a few outdid them. If one measures depth and originality of thought, it is difficult to find a Parisian who compares with Hume, Smith, Burke, Winckelmann, Kant, and Goethe. Why then concentrate on Paris?

That is where the movement came together and defined itself as a cause. In an earlier phase, one that I would call the pre-Enlightenment, philosophic writers like John Locke, John Toland, and Pierre Bayle crossed paths throughout England and the Low Countries. They shared itineraries and ideas, including Bayle's vision of an international Republic of Letters. But it was not until their intellectual heirs, the *philosophes*, set up camp and began campaigning that the Enlightenment emerged as a cause, with partisans and a program. Its adherents forged their collective identity in Paris during the first decades of the eighteenth century. As their movement gathered force, it spread, and as it spread, it changed, adapting itself to other conditions and incorporating other ideas. But it did not reach everywhere and cover everything in the spectrum of intellectual life. To equate the Enlightenment with the totality of Western thought in the eighteenth century is to get it badly wrong. By viewing it as a concerted campaign on the part of a self-conscious group of intellectuals, one can reduce it to its proper proportions. This perspective does justice to its character, for the *philosophes* concentrated less on developing systematic philosophy than on mastering the media of their time. They excelled in witty conversation, letter writing, manuscript bulletins, journalism, and all forms of the printed word, from the massive tomes of the *Encyclopédie* to the pamphlet *pâtés* served up by Voltaire.

The diffusionist view also allows for the spread of the Enlightenment to other parts of Europe in the second half of the eighteenth century and to the rest of the world thereafter. By 1750 like-minded philosophers in other sites had begun to think of themselves as *philosophes*. Paris drew them like a magnet, and the Parisians enlisted them in the cause, delighted to find reinforcement from original thinkers like Hume and Beccaria. But the foreign *philosophe*, with his imperfect French and incorrectly curled wig, felt his foreignness in Paris. He often returned home determined to strike out on his own. (Despite the lionizing in Paris, Beccaria hustled back to Milan as fast as his coach would carry him and turned from criminology to aesthetics.) The *philosophe en mission* in London, Berlin, and Milan also discovered alien sources of thought, many of them distressingly Christian. Fissures opened; divisions developed; branches stretched out in new directions. Such is the nature of movements. They are always in motion, multiplying and dividing.

An emphasis on diffusion does not imply indifference to ideas, either among the *philosophes* or among the historians studying them. Nor does it imply passivity on the receiving end of the messages sent out from Paris and from other transmission points along the circuits of intellectual exchange. On the contrary, the foreigners talked back. Backtalk, personal interaction, mutual exchange of letters and books kept expanding "the Church," as Voltaire called it. And the cause carried conviction because the ideas of the *philosophes* were *idées-forces*, like liberty, happiness, nature, and nature's laws.

But they were not particularly original. Thinkers in Stockholm and Naples did not need to read Voltaire in order to learn about tolerance and natural law.

Those ideas belonged to the common stock of concepts accessible to the educated classes everywhere. Philosophers worked them over in new ways without any need for nudging from Paris and often without any alignment with the Enlightenment. What Voltaire and his coconspirators provided was not original matter for thought but a new spirit, the sense of participation in a secular crusade. It began with derision, as an attempt to laugh the bigots out of polite society, and it ended with the occupation of the moral high ground, as a campaign for the liberation of mankind, including the enserfed and the enslaved, Protestants, Jews, blacks, and (in the case of Condorcet) women.

From deflation to diffusion and diffusion to the study of a spirit, this approach to the Enlightenment may well seem suspect. For if we are not to make an inventory of ideas but rather to take the pulse of a movement, will we not be forced to rely on groping in the dark for a *Zeitgeist*? I prefer to think that we can pursue a more rigorous historicity. Movements can be mapped. One can follow them in space and time, as groups cohere and messages flow through communication systems.

The Enlightenment grew out of a great crisis during the last years of the reign of Louis XIV. For a century the power of the monarchy and the prestige of literature had grown apace, but after 1685 they grew apart. The Revocation of the Edict of Nantes, the quarrel of the Ancients and Moderns, the persecution of Jansenists and Quietists all came to a head while France suffered through a series of demographic, economic, and military disasters. With the state on the verge of collapse, men of letters attached to the court—Fénelon, La Bruyère, Boulainvilliers, Vauban, Saint-Simon—questioned the basis of Bourbon absolutism and the religious orthodoxy it enforced. *La ville* went its own way as *la cour* succumbed to paralysis, waiting for the death of the aged king. A new generation of *esprits forts* and *beaux esprits* took over the salons and breathed new life into the libertinism developed during the seventeenth century. In 1706 a twelve-year-old prodigy, François-Marie Arouet, later known as Voltaire, made his debut in the libertine society of the Temple. By the death of Louis XIV nine years later he had established a reputation as the sharpest wit in town, and the town, or the wealthy, worldly part of it known as *le monde*, had given itself over to witticisms, most of them at the expense of the Church and whatever passed for dignity in the governing circles of the Regency.

The Enlightenment at this stage remained confined to a narrow elite and also to word of mouth and manuscript. *Bons mots* and libertine tracts passed from salon to salon, but they rarely appeared in print. The first great exceptions were Montesquieu's *Lettres Persanes* (1721) and Voltaire's *Lettres philosophiques* (1734). Both works showed an advance from wit to wisdom, for both authors mixed libertine impieties with serious reflections on despotism and intolerance. Having been beaten up by the lackeys of the chevalier de Rohan-Chabot and imprisoned twice in the Bastille, Voltaire had learned to appreciate the weakness of independent writers in a world dominated by protection networks of wealth and birth.

The next great publishing event, the appearance of *Le Philosophe* in 1743, provided an answer to that problem. Writers should conform to an ideal type: neither a scientist nor a savant, but a new phenomenon, the *philosophe*, part man of letters, part man of the world, and entirely engaged in using letters to rid the world of superstition. This little tract, later incorporated in the *Encyclopédie* and in Voltaire's *Évangile de la raison*, served as a declaration of independence for the intellectual and at the same time provided him with a strategy: He should work within the power structure, promoting an alliance of *gens de lettres* and *gens du monde*, in order to advance the cause of *philosophie*.

The *philosophes*, as the group now began to be known, found their greatest ally in C. G. de Lamoignon de Malesherbes, the director of the book trade from 1750 to 1763. Thanks to his protection, the Enlightenment burst fully into print. Despite persecution from clergymen and magistrates, the most important works, from Montesquieu's *De l'esprit des lois* (1748) to Rousseau's *Émile* and *Du contrat social* (1762), circulated safely through the arteries of the publishing industry. The *Encyclopédie* (seventeen volumes of text, 1751–1765, followed by eleven volumes of plates, the last published in 1772) redefined the world of knowledge for the modern reader, infused it with *philosophie*, and identified it with a coterie of *philosophes*, the *société de gens de lettres* named on its title page. The *Encyclopédie* caused a scandal and nearly went under; but by 1789 it had become the greatest best seller in the history of publishing. Despite some hard knocks, or rather because of them, particularly during the political-intellectual crisis of 1757–1762, the *philosophe* had emerged as a new social type and a force to be reckoned with, the phenomenon that we now identify as the intellectual.

The rest of the story need not be related here. It has plenty of complexities and contradictions (not the least of which was Jean-Jacques Rousseau), and it can hardly be reduced to a tranquil process of diffusing light by selling books. After the 1750s most of it took place outside France, especially through the recasting of autocratic power in the form of enlightened absolutism. But everywhere—in the Prussia of Frederick II, the Russia of Catherine II, the Austria of Joseph II, the Tuscany of the archduke Leopold, the Spain of Charles III, the Portugal of Joseph I, the Sweden of Gustavus III—sovereigns and ministers looked to the *philosophes* for guidance or legitimation. Nearly all of them read French; nearly all

consulted the *Encyclopédie*, and so did the most important of their
subjects.

The point of taking this detour through historicism is not merely
to reduce the Enlightenment to manageable proportions but also to
address the next question, its relevance to issues that arose after the
eighteenth century. The inflated Enlightenment can be identified
with all modernity, with nearly everything subsumed under the
name of Western civilization, and so it can be made responsible for
nearly everything that causes discontent, especially in the camps of
the postmodernists and anti-Westernizers.

II

Whatever our success in shrinking the Enlightenment down to its
true size as an eighteenth-century phenomenon, we cannot deny
that it produced a set of values that remained alive through the centuries that followed and that set some societies apart from others.
The nomenclature varies—modern vs. medieval, bourgeois vs.
aristocratic, liberal vs. traditional, capitalist vs. feudal—but taken
together, the contrasting terms point to a dividing line that has long
existed in the collective consciousness. Like most boundaries, it has
provoked conflict. Some have wanted to move it; some, to wipe it
out. Now, however, it may simply disappear without a fight because
a new line has been drawn: 1989, the demarcation of two eras—
before and after the Cold War. We have come to the end of a short
century, which extended from 1914 to 1989, but we do not know
what century we have entered.

The age of postmodernism? The term means different things to
different people, but however unsatisfactory it may be, it conveys a
sense of rupture from a time when the terms were clear or at least
clearly strung out along a set of opposites. One was for or against

liberalism, conservatism, capitalism, socialism, individualism, collectivism, and so on. Now we talk, or rather discourse, about representing, remembering, inventing, negotiating, construing, constructing, and deconstructing. Having taken the linguistic turn, we feel free to reedit reality and to pronounce the Enlightenment dead. But reality refuses to behave like a text, and the Enlightenment seems to have life in it yet, because it is still a whipping boy, and one doesn't whip cadavers. The attacks have changed, however. In place of the old accusations—shallow positivism, naive optimism, bourgeois ideology—postmodernists have arraigned the Enlightenment under a new set of headings. The indictment goes as follows:

1. The Enlightenment's claim to universalism really served as a cover for Western hegemony. The rights of man provided legitimation for the destruction of other cultures. Example: Captain Cook.

I would not minimize the damage wrought by Westerners when they came into contact with other parts of the world, nor would I dispute Cook's reputation as a prototypical man of the Enlightenment. But Cook showed much respect for native customs, far more than the conquistadors of the sixteenth century and the imperialists of the nineteenth. Tragedy could not be avoided in the West-East and North-South encounters, but it was driven by trade, disease, and technology rather than by philosophy. Mutual incomprehension certainly compounded the damage. Its cultural dimension was crucial; but the Enlightenment was not the same thing as Western culture, and the *philosophes* made laudable efforts not only to understand other peoples but also to improve their lot: thus the *Histoire philosophique des établissements et du commerce des Européens dans les deux Indes*, a radical and widely diffused tract by the abbé Raynal, which contributed greatly to the abolition of slavery.

A related accusation goes somewhat differently:

2. The Enlightenment was cultural imperialism masquerading as

a higher form of rationality. It provided Europeans with a "civilizing mission" and a way of constructing "natives" that led to their silencing and subjugation. Example: Orientalism.

This argument draws on Foucault, literary theory, and anthropology to emphasize the epistemological and cultural ingredients in Western hegemony. No one who has read through those sources would deny that individuals are always construing others. In cross-cultural contacts, "othering" (as the jargon would have it) can be fatal. It leads to "essentialism" (another current pejorative)—that is, the projection of qualities on others in a way that reifies them in the eyes of the beholder and sometimes in their own eyes as well. In this respect Enlightenment thought can look "culture-bound" and "nondialogical" (two more taboos in postmodern social science). But every culture has boundaries. Western notions of individualism may indeed be incompatible with the notions of selfhood developed in China and India. But the Enlightenment opened the way to an anthropological understanding of others. It was deeply dialogical and provided an antidote to its own tendency to dogmatize: Witness Diderot's *Supplément au Voyage de Bougainville* and all his dialogues.

Orientalism certainly provided the Westerners with stereotypes that they visited on the East, and the *philosophes* contributed their share to this tendency. Montesquieu and Voltaire may have put their sympathetic Persians and philosophical Chinese in a positive light in order to project criticisms back on France; but positive stereotyping is stereotyping, nonetheless, and it may close off receptivity to any genuine give-and-take with other cultures. But other ages, in contrast with the eighteenth century, were nearly all take and no give. Imperialism is essentially a nineteenth-century phenomenon, and it took its inspiration from the Romantics rather than the *philosophes*. Byron and Kipling, Delacroix and Ingres, Verdi and Puccini outdid the artists of the eighteenth century by far in creating exotic Orientals. Moreover, the exoticizing began long before the Enlightenment, and it often took the form of demonizing. Cruel Saracens, Oriental despots, and *têtes de Turcs* have proliferated in the Western imagination since the early wars against the Ottoman Empire. Older prejudices date from the Crusades. They developed over centuries, accompanied, it must be said, by Eastern prejudices against the West. (After I heard a paper on the reception of Rousseau in Japan, it seemed to me that we should consider "Occidentalism" as well as "Orientalism.") To pin Orientalism on the Enlightenment is to confuse the thought of a few intellectuals in the eighteenth century with the entire course of Western civilization.

Finally, it must be stressed that the Enlightenment lacked the most poisonous ingredient of imperialism—namely, racism. There is no getting around Jefferson's support of slavery or the biological speculations by Lord Kames and Lord Monboddo on the nature of Amerindians, Africans, and Orang Outangs. But for more typical views, one should turn to the passionate denunciation of slavery by Voltaire in *Candide,* Chapter 19, which was inspired by the radical egalitarianism of Helvétius's *De l'esprit*. Race was not a fundamental category in the thought of the *philosophes*. The world had to wait for the likes of Gobineau to arrive at that level of philosophy.

3. The Enlightenment pursued knowledge so fanatically that it undermined ethics. Ultimately that fanaticism fed into fascism, because it armed the state with superior technology and destroyed the moral barriers to the all-pervasive exercise of state power. Newton's natural law became reduced to matter in motion, despite his faith in an interventionist, Christian God. Kant's "dare to know" became "dare to reject the promptings of the conscience" despite his attempt to provide a rational basis for the Golden Rule. The *philosophes* did not merely damage organized religion; they also

sapped all morality, which ultimately rests on the irrational: faith and Revelation. Example: the marquis de Sade.

Sade has indeed been presented as the ultimate *philosophe*, the one who put d'Alembert's "experimental physics of the soul" into practice in the darkest corners of cruelty. Max Horkheimer and Theodor Adorno aligned Sade with Kant and Nietzsche in a "dialectic of enlightenment" that stretched from Homer to Hitler. Faced with the disasters of totalitarianism and world war, they questioned the assumed wisdom of the Left, which associated Enlightenment with revolution. Instead they argued that the Enlightenment led by a negative dialectic to what might seem to be its opposite, fascism.

One can see their point: Rational demystification of the eighteenth-century sort might be understood to produce its dialectical opposite, a modern mythology of science and technology, which opened onto a moral wilderness. But can one take it seriously as an account of the Enlightenment? Horkheimer and Adorno do not discuss the work of a single French *philosophe*. Instead of considering the Enlightenment concretely, as a phenomenon located in time and space, they let it disappear from sight while speculating on the entire sweep of Western civilization.

The blind spot in their speculations has serious consequences because the Enlightenment provided the main defense against the barbarism that they deplored. Montesquieu's attempt to shore up liberty against the inroads of despotism, Voltaire's campaigns against the perversions of justice, Rousseau's plea for the rights of the dispossessed, Diderot's questioning of all authority, including that of reason itself: Such were the weapons left by the intellectuals of the eighteenth century for their successors two hundred years later. Horkheimer and Adorno refused to make use of them.

Instead they drew on another philosophical tradition, the one that leads from Hegel to Heidegger. Not that they subscribed to Heidegger's Hitlerism. But by viewing Hitler from the perspective of German dialectics, they were incapable of making sense of the supreme evil that overcame Germany. That evil stands condemned by the standards of human rights developed in the Enlightenment and proclaimed in the founding charters of democracy, notably the American Declaration of Independence and the French Declaration of the Rights of Man and of the Citizen. There may be inadequate evidence for the "self-evident truths" of the American Declaration. They are articles of faith, not facts. But one must put one's faith somewhere—better, I believe, in the normative tradition of the Enlightenment than in the dialectics designed to refute it.

4. The Enlightenment had an excessive faith in reason. By relying on rationalism, it failed to erect defenses against the irrational. Its naive cult of progress left humanity helpless before the horrors of the twentieth century.

Faith in reason is indeed a faith, and it may not be adequate to sustain men and women confronted with the violence and irrationality of the twentieth century. But rationalism does not distinguish the Enlightenment from other schools of thought, such as Thomism or Cartesianism. The pertinent distinction, as Ernst Cassirer explained, sets apart the *esprit systématique* of the eighteenth century from the *esprit de système* of the seventeenth. The latter carried reason to extremes by using it to construct all-embracing theories. The *philosophes* challenged theories. They dared criticize everything, but with very few exceptions—d'Holbach, Quesnay—they did not erect systems.

What is the alternative to the critical use of reason? Embracing the irrational? Freud relied on reason in order to explore the irrational. He followed the lead of Diderot, whose *Neveu de Rameau* provides a clinical case study of a man without morality, who wanted to kill his father so that he could sleep with his mother. Nietzsche celebrated the Dionysian ingredient in culture, but he admired Voltaire and did not provide a rationale for his postmod-

ernist followers to abandon the Voltairean struggle against tyranny
and social injustice.

The most typical of the postmodernist attacks on the Enlightenment, John Gray's *Enlightenment's Wake*, invokes Nietzsche in urging
us to abandon faith in normative principles and to accept the neces-
sity of taking up stands in a landscape shorn of meaningful markers.
Like Horkheimer and Adorno, Gray does not pause to consider
what the French *philosophes* actually wrote. Instead he offers a vague
and unsubstantiated description of something he calls the enlightenment project and proceeds to condemn it for its failure to meet
the standards set by postmodernist philosophy. Aside from its
anachronism, the argument seems to assume that political culture
derives from political theory, as if a wrong turn or a twist in the
logic of a philosopher could determine the way ordinary mortals
orient themselves in the world. Gray sets them straight. Armed
with arguments from Nietzsche, Horkheimer, and Adorno, he
slashes away at what he takes to be the Enlightenment world view,
leaves it in tatters, and challenges his readers to accept their "historical fate"—that is, the world according to Gray, a world without
enlightenment, "the postmodern condition of fractured perspectives and groundless practices."[1]

The philosophers of the Enlightenment probably would fail that
test if Gray administered it after considering their work. Condorcet—distracted, no doubt, from an understanding of historical
fate by his efforts to free slaves, enfranchise women, and stop
Robespierre—probably would get an F, for what could look more
groundless, when viewed from this side of Hitlerism and Stalinism,
than his theory of progress: reason driving out falsehood with help
from the printing press? But it may not be absurd to envision
progress with a lowercase *p,* of which more later. Meanwhile what
should we make of the combination of reason and Terror, which
drove Condorcet to suicide?

5. The Enlightenment belongs to the origins of totalitarianism. It provided the theoretical basis for the Terror of the French Revolution, which in turn pointed the way to the terrors of Hitler and Stalin. The common element in all three was the attempt to force the social order to conform to an ideological blueprint.

True, in making his case for the Terror, Robespierre drew on Montesquieu and Rousseau. Like many other Jacobins, he tried to redesign France in accordance with political theory. But he also smashed the bust of Helvétius in the Jacobin Club and railed against the Encyclopedists, reserving his praise for the one *philosophe*, Rousseau, who made a break with the Enlightenment and opened the way to Romanticism. Rousseau's notion of forcing men to be free by making them conform to the dictates of an organic General Will undercut the notions of liberty developed by the other *philosophes*. But Rousseau never envisaged anything like the Terror, and the Terror had nothing in common with the ideologies of fascism and communism. The crimes committed by twentieth-century states violated basic principles of the Enlightenment: respect for the individual, for liberty, for all the rights of man.

But rhetoric about the rights of man exposes the Enlightenment to a further critique: It says nothing about the rights of women. And what about animals, the environment, and other causes that command the attention of the post–Cold War world? Those questions lead to a final accusation.

6. The Enlightenment is outdated and inadequate as an outlook for coping with contemporary problems. The *philosophes* championed an instrumentalist view of reason, which led to ecological disaster, and a masculine view of civic life, which relegated women to the private sphere.

True, the Enlightenment was time-bound as well as culture-bound. It took place in a world where some causes of the twentieth century remained unthinkable. It therefore failed to think great

thoughts that later changed the boundaries of culture. To defend the
Enlightenment is not to reject the poetry of T. S. Eliot, the painting
of Picasso, the physics of Einstein, or even the grammatology of
Derrida. Nor is it to reject the rights of women. Olympe de
Gouges and Mary Wollstonecraft actually owed a great deal to the
example as well as to the ideas of the *philosophes*, even though some
speculations of Diderot and Rousseau seem retrogressive when
compared with the earlier notions of Poulain de la Barre. The point
is not to make an inventory of ideas, crossing some off the list and
adding others. It is to adopt an intellectual stance that will serve
when lines are drawn and one's back is to the wall. When challenged to condemn torture in Argentina, war in Vietnam, or racism
in the United States, where can we make our stand if not on principles enshrined in the Declaration of Independence and the Declaration of the Rights of Man and of the Citizen?

Having come to the end of the indictment, I realize that I have
fallen into the role of an advocate and abandoned that of a historian.
Historians often succumb to such slippage when they belong to the
culture they study. Why not throw professionalism to the wind and
slide all the way into sermonizing?

III

If I may add some observations of my own, I would stress the
refusal of the *philosophes* to respect boundaries, either of disciplines
or of nations. Despite their Parisian origins and their proclivity for
French, they lived in a Republic of Letters that was truly cosmopolitan. It had neither borders nor police. It was open to ideas from
everywhere. Yet no one in it, or anywhere else, conceived of the
idea of nationalism. That barbarism began with the wars of 1792
and the fatal notion of "My country, right or wrong!"

I recently strayed out of the eighteenth century in order to do some research on the British Raj in the archives of the India Office in London. Before long my ears were ringing with a refrain that appeared in all the documents. *Bande Mataram! Bande Mataram! Bande Mataram* ("Long live the Mother!"—that is, India) was the rallying cry of the Indian revolutionaries who wanted to throw off the *Feringhees* ("foreigners") at the beginning of this century. It was their Liberty, Equality, Fraternity. It moved them to tears, occasionally even to suicidal bomb attacks. And its fascination, to a *Feringhee*, is its unthinkability. What is *Bande Mataram* to me?

And Liberty, Equality, Fraternity? Two centuries of bad weather have nearly worn the words off the faces of most town halls in France. I doubt that they resonate inside the souls of many French today. You hear them, if at all, in parody: "Neither Liberty, nor Equality, nor Fraternity, but a little more mustard, *s'il vous plaît*." The last time I noticed a patriotic lump in a French throat was at a screening of *Casablanca*, when Humphrey Bogart got the crowd to sing the "Marseillaise."

Yet only yesterday men were killing one another for a few square kilometers of Bosnia. To die for Greater Serbia? Another unthinkable thought. For a United Ireland? Only recenty has the IRA agreed to stop throwing bombs. The ETA bomb throwers still kill in the name of the Basque Fatherland. Kurds assassinate in Turkey, Palestinians in Israel, Israelis in Palestine, Tamils in Sri Lanka, all for rearrangements of the map. The same thing is going on in Cyprus, Azerbaijan, Chechnya. . . .

No need to recite the entire list. We all know it well enough. What we do not and cannot take in is the passion that drives men to kill for such causes. For us, the tiny minority of well-fed, well-educated Westerners, Robert Graves said it all at the end of World War I: "Goodbye to all that." Our fathers fought in World War II to extinguish nationalism, not to unleash it. Yet every day it explodes before our eyes on the screens of our television sets. How can we make sense of the drive to die for fantasies like Mother India?

Here is Ajit Singh, a passionate nationalist, haranguing a crowd at Rawalpindi in 1907, according to a police agent who secretly took down his words: "Die for your country. We are 30 crores [300,000,000]. They are a lakh and a half [150,000]. A puff of wind would blow them away. Cannon are of no account. One finger can easily be broken. When five fingers join to make a fist, no one can break it. (This was given with great emphasis, and flowers were thrown.)"

One gets the point. But can one "get" the gale of flowers, the stamping of bare feet, the songs bursting from chests, the small boys rushing to take oaths in blood, the old men with tears in their eyes, the lumps in all the throats?

The words remain, the music has gone—at least for those of us who respond to Graves and would add: "Goodbye and good riddance! May nationalism die a thousand deaths and never rise again." Yet there it is, alive and howling all around us, practically within hearing distance of London, Amsterdam, Paris, and Rome. Is there any way we can pick up the beat, if not in sympathy, at least with enough empathy to understand the force that drives it?

One way lies through a reconsideration of our own traditions. We may be appalled at the patriotic gore spread throughout our past, but even the most sophisticated of us, at one time or other, has felt that peculiar lump in the throat.

I underwent an attack of lumpiness myself, I must confess, during a guided tour of Independence Hall in Philadelphia a few years ago. There sat Washington, the guide explained, in that very chair, in this very room. It was a handsome Georgian chair with an emblematic sun carved on its back, and Washington was presiding over the Constitutional Convention of 1787. At a particularly difficult moment in the debates, when the fate of the young republic seemed to hang in the balance, Benjamin Franklin, sitting here, asked George Mason, sitting there, "Is the sun rising or setting?" They got through that deadlock and a dozen others. And when at last they had completed their work, Franklin pronounced: "It is rising."

"What great men they were," I said to myself, the lump growing in my throat. "Washington, Franklin, Madison—and Jefferson, at that moment advising Lafayette during the first phase of the French Revolution. How much greater than our politicians today. They were men of the Enlightenment."

I cannot comprehend the rising sun of Japan, and I doubt that Washington's sun meant much to the Japanese tourists at my side in Independence Hall. Seen from abroad, the cult of the Constitution and the Founding Fathers must look like an alien folklore. To be sure, Washington himself no longer stirs much emotion in American breasts. Unlike Lincoln and Roosevelt, he looks too stiff, propped up in those Gilbert Stuart portraits, jaw firm, lips pursed, brow ponderous, more an icon than a human being. Icons are for worshiping, but the iconic Washington worshiped in the United States is the one that looks out at us from the dollar bill.

Now, the cult of the dollar may not be all bad. Its emotional range is limited but not lethal. Unlike nationalism, it inspires self-interest rather than self-sacrifice, investment rather than bomb throwing. And for all its crassness, it is ecumenical; one man's dollar is as good as another's. That principle also derives from the Enlightenment, the branch that runs through Mandeville and Adam Smith. Enlightened self-interest may not be as lofty as Liberty, Equality, Fraternity; but it made a new life possible in the New World for millions of immigrants, and it may ultimately renovate Russia, where the dollar has become the effective currency.

This line of thought has a respectable ancestry. It passed through French physiocracy, Scottish moral philosophy, and English utilitarianism. But it takes us Americans far away from the passions that inspired our ancestors in the early nineteenth century, when they carved, painted, sewed, and spun images of Washington into everything they produced. If we cannot share that emotion, we may nonetheless learn something by catching a glimpse of the man behind the icon.

Once, on a visit to Washington's estate at Mount Vernon, I ran across what must be one of the strangest relics ever displayed in a national shrine, stranger than all the bric-a-brac in the Lenin Museum of Moscow and the Wellington Museum of London, Washington's false teeth. There they sat, under glass and (as I then believed) made of wood! The Father of Our Country in wooden choppers! So that was why he looked so grim in the portraits. The man was in constant pain. He couldn't get any juice from his meat without sending shock waves through his gums.

People often ask me, as a specialist in the field, Would I like to have lived in the eighteenth century? First, I say, I would insist on being born well above the peasantry. Second, no toothaches, please. While reading thousands of letters from people in all walks of eighteenth-century life, I have often encountered toothaches. The pain cuts through the archaic language, and the writer looms up in your imagination, waiting in dread for an itinerant tooth puller to arrive in town and, by a brief bout of torture, to put an end to the long weeks of agony.

Today we have less toothache and more mustard, much of it first-rate, from Dijon. Can we call this Progress? That is another eighteenth-century idea that looks dubious when seen across two centuries of suffering. But some familiarity with what humanity has suffered in the past may help us appreciate the modest, incremental gains of pleasure over pain or progress with a lowercase *p*. It may also help us sympathize with those who took a stand for human rights in the face of inhumanity. I am thinking of Voltaire, not the young libertine but the angry old man, who threw all his last energy into the fight against fanaticism. If he seems too foreign for postmodern America, why not summon up the central figure in our own political culture? When the crunch comes, we may be able to face up to the injustices around us by gritting our teeth and remembering how hard it was for Washington to grit his.

2

THE NEWS IN PARIS:
AN EARLY INFORMATION
SOCIETY

FROM THE THRESHOLD OF THE TWENTY-FIRST CENTURY, IT
APPEARS THAT THE ROAD TO THE NEW MILLENNIUM LEADS
THROUGH SILICON VALLEY. We have entered the information age,
and the future, it seems, will be determined by the media. In fact
some would claim that the modes of communication have replaced
the modes of production as the driving force of the modern world.
I should like to dispute that view. Whatever its value as prophecy, it
will not work as history because it conveys a specious sense of a
break with the past. I would argue that every age was an age of
information, each in its own way, and that communication systems
have always shaped events.[1]

   That argument may sound suspiciously like common sense, but
if pushed hard enough, it could open up a fresh perspective on the
past. As a starting point, I would ask a question about the media
today: What is news? Most of us would reply that news is what we
read in newspapers or see and hear on news broadcasts. If we considered the matter further, however, we probably would agree that
news is not what happened—yesterday, or last week—but rather
stories about what happened. It is a kind of narrative, transmitted
by special kinds of media. That line of reasoning soon leads to
entanglement in literary theory and the World Wide Web. But if

projected backward, it may help disentangle some knotty problems in the past.[2]

I would propose a general attack on the problem of how societies made sense of events and transmitted information about them, something that might be called the history of communication. In principle, this kind of history could provoke a reassessment of any period in the past, for every society develops its own ways of hunting and gathering information; its means of communicating what it gathers, whether or not it uses concepts such as news and the media, can reveal a great deal about its understanding of its own experience. Examples can be cited from studies of coffeehouses in Stuart England, teahouses in early republican China, marketplaces in contemporary Morocco, street poetry in seventeenth-century Rome, slave rebellions in nineteenth-century Brazil, runner networks in the Mogul Raj of India, even the bread and circuses of the Roman Empire.[3]

But instead of attempting to pile up examples by roaming everywhere through the historical record, I should like to examine a communication system at work in a particular time and place, the Old Regime in France. More precisely I would ask, How did you find out what the news was in Paris around 1750? Not, I submit, by reading a newspaper, because papers with news in them—news as we understand it today, about public affairs and prominent persons—did not exist. The government did not permit them.

To find out what was really going on, you went to the Tree of Cracow. It was a large, leafy chestnut tree, which stood at the heart of Paris in the gardens of the Palais-Royal. It probably had acquired its name from heated discussions that took place around it during the War of the Polish Succession (1733–1735), although the name also suggested rumormongering (*craquer:* to tell dubious stories). Like a mighty magnet, the tree attracted *nouvellistes de bouche,* or newsmongers, who spread information about current events by

word of mouth. They claimed to know, from private sources (a letter, an indiscreet servant, a remark overheard in an antechamber of
Versailles), what was really happening in the corridors of power,
and the people in power took them seriously because the government worried about what Parisians were saying. Foreign diplomats
allegedly sent agents to pick up news or to plant it at the foot of the
Tree of Cracow. (See Figures 2 and 3.) There were several other
nerve centers for transmitting "public noises" (*bruits publics*), as this
variety of news was known: special benches in the Tuileries and
Luxembourg Gardens (see Figure 4), informal speakers' corners
on the Quai des Augustins and the Pont-Neuf, cafés known for their
loose talk, and boulevards where news bulletins were bawled out
by peddlers of *canards* (facetious broadsides) or sung by
hurdy-gurdy players. To tune in on the news, you could simply
stand in the street and cock your ear.[4]

But ordinary hearsay did not satisfy Parisians with a powerful
appetite for information. They needed to sift through the public
noise in order to discover what was *really* happening. Sometimes
they pooled their information and criticized it collectively by meeting in groups such as the famous salon of Mme. M.-A. L. Doublet,
known as "the parish." Twenty-nine "parishioners," many of them
well connected with the Parlement of Paris or the court and all of
them famished for news, gathered once a week in Mme. Doublet's
apartment in the Enclos des Filles Saint-Thomas. When they
entered the salon, they reportedly found two large registers on a
desk near the door. One contained news reputed to be reliable; the
other, gossip. Together they constituted the menu for the day's discussion, which was prepared by one of Mme. Doublet's servants,
who may qualify as the first "reporter" in the history of France. We
don't know his name, but a description of him survives in the files
of the police (and I should say at the outset that police archives provide most of the evidence I draw on here—important evidence, I

Fig. 2. Detail from an engraving after M. Peyrotte's "Council of Monkeys: Dedicated to Messieurs the *nouvellistes* of the Tree of Cracow." Courtesy of the Bibliothèque nationale de France. This satirical print shows newsmongers (*nouvellistes*) at a favorite gathering place for a public reading of a report about a battle, possibly during the War of the Polish Succession, 1733–1735. One monkey *nouvelliste* draws a figure in the sand to illustrate the alignment of troops. The others listen and comment with a knowing air, as if they could debate foreign affairs with all the expertise of genuine statesmen. Public commentary would no longer appear ridiculous in the 1780s, when foreign affairs, like all the activities of the government, were exposed to "the tribunal of public opinion," as it was commonly called.

believe, but the kind that calls for especially critical interpretation): He was "tall and fat, a full face, round wig, and a brown outfit. Every morning he goes from house to house asking, in the name of his mistress, 'What's new?'"[5] The servant wrote the first entries for

each day's news on the registers; the "parishioners" read through
them, adding whatever other information they had gathered; and
after a general vetting, the reports were copied and sent to select
friends of Mme. Doublet. One of them, J.-G. Bosc du Bouchet,

comtesse d'Argental, had a lackey named Gillet, who organized
another copying service. When he began to make money by selling
the copies—provincial subscribers gladly paid six livres a month to
keep up with the latest news from Paris—some of his copyists set
up shops of their own, and those shops spawned other shops, so that
by 1750 multiple editions of Mme. Doublet's newsletter were fly-
ing around Paris and the provinces. The copying operations—an
efficient means of diffusion long after Gutenberg and long before
Xerox—had turned into a minor industry, a news service provid-
ing subscribers with manuscript gazettes, or *nouvelles à la main.*

1. La Vérité.) 2. un Cabartier qui ne frelatte point, Crac.) 3. un Marchand qui vend en Conscience, Crac.)
  sans prevention, Crac) 6. un Abbé qui ne minaude point, Crac.) 7. un petit Maitre modeste, Crac.) 8. une Danseuse
servante Champenoise Sage, Crac.) 10. un Gascon opulent, Crac.) 11. un Astrologue qui voit Clair, Crac.) 12. un
sobre, Crac.) 14. un Caissier humble et poli, Crac.) 15. des Nouvellistes sans partialité, Crac.) 16. un Architecte hab
  contrefaction, Crac, Crac.) 18. des Filles toujours amies, Crac.) 19. un Ecolier assidu à l'Etude Crac) 20. un I

In 1777 publishers began putting these *nouvelles* into print, and they circulated as the *Mémoires secrets pour servir à l'histoire de la République des Lettres en France,* a best seller in the underground book trade.[6]

Anecdotal as they are, these examples show that news (*nouvelles*) circulated through several media and by different modes—oral, manuscript, and print. In each case, moreover, it remained outside the law. So we also should consider the political constraints on the news.

This is a rich and complicated subject because research during the last twenty years has transformed the history of early modern journalism.[7] Simplifying radically, I would insist on a basic point: Information about the inner workings of the power system was not supposed to circulate under the Old Regime in France. Politics was the king's business, *le secret du roi,* a notion derived from a late medieval and Renaissance view, which treated statecraft as *arcana imperii,* a secret art restricted to sovereigns and their advisers.[8]

. un Maquignon veridique,Crac)5.un Poëte
ui ne fait point de faux pas,Crac,Crac)9.une
intre sans Caprice,Crac)13, un Musicien
'e sans être guindé,Crac)17.un Graveur sans
endant de maison qui à les mains nettes,Crac

Fig. 3. "L'Arbre de Cracovie," c. 1742. The Tree of Cracow as depicted in a satirical print. The figure of Truth, on the far left, pulls on a rope to make the tree go "crack" every time something false takes place beneath it. According to the caption, the falsehoods include an innkeeper who claims he does not water down his wine, a merchant who sells goods for no more than what they are worth, a truthful horse dealer, an unbiased poet, etc. Courtesy of the Bibliothèque nationale de France (BNF), 96A 74336.

Fig. 4. A group of *nouvellistes* discussing the news in the Luxembourg Gardens. Courtesy of the BNF, 88C 134231.

Of course some information reached the reading public through journals and gazettes, but it was not supposed to deal with the inside story of politics or with politics at all, except in the form of official pronouncements on court life. All printed matter had to be cleared through a baroque bureaucracy that included nearly two hundred censors, and the censors' decisions were enforced by a special branch of the police, the inspectors of the book trade. The inspectors did not merely repress heresy and sedition; they also protected privileges. Official journals—notably the *Gazette de France, Mercure,* and *Journal des savants*—possessed royal privileges for the coverage of certain subjects, and no new periodical could be established without paying them for a share in their turf. When the revolutionaries looked back at the history of the press, they saw nothing but newslessness before 1789. Thus Pierre Manuel on the *Gazette de France:*

A people that wants to be informed cannot be satisfied with the *Gazette de France.* Why should it care if the king has performed the ritual of foot-washing for some poor folk whose feet weren't even dirty? Or if the queen celebrated Easter in company with the comte d'Artois? Or if Monsieur deigned to accept the dedication of a book that he may never read? Or if the Parlement, dressed in ceremonial attire, harangued the baby dauphin, who was dressed in swaddling clothes? The people want to know everything that is actually done and said in the court—why and for whom the cardinal de Rohan should have taken it into his head to play games with a pearl necklace; if it is true that the comtesse Diane appoints the generals of the army and the comtesse Jule the bishops; how many Saint Louis medals the minister of war allotted to his mistress for distribution as New Year's presents. It was the sharp-witted authors of clandestine gazettes [*nouvelles à la main*] who spread the word about this kind of scandal.[9]

These remarks, written at the height of the excitement over a newly freed press, exaggerate the servility of journalism under the

Old Regime. Many periodicals existed, many of them printed in French outside France, and they sometimes provided information about political events, especially during the relatively liberal reign of Louis XVI (1774–1792). But if any ventured criticism of the government, they could easily be snuffed out by the police—not simply by raids on bookshops and arrests of peddlers, which frequently occurred, but by being excluded from the mail. Distribution through the mail left their supply lines very vulnerable, as the *Gazette de Leyde* learned when it tried and failed to cover the most important political story of Louis XV's reign, the destruction of the parlements from 1771 to 1774.

So newspapers of a sort existed, but they had little news, and the reading public had little faith in them, not even in the French journals that arrived from Holland. The general skepticism was expressed clearly in a report from a police spy in 1746:

> It is openly said that France pays 2,000 livres [a year] to Sieur du Breuil, author of the *Gazette d'Amsterdam,* which is vetted by the French representative at The Hague. Besides that, France gives 12,000 to 15,000 livres to Mme. Limiers, who does the *Gazette d'Utrecht.* This money comes from the revenue of the gazettes, which the postal service sells for 17 sous 6 deniers [per copy] to David, its distributor in Paris, and which he sells to the public for 20 sous. When the gazettes did not appear as usual yesterday, it was said that the minister had had them stopped.[10]

In short, the press was far from free, and it was also underdeveloped, if you compare it with the press in Holland, England, and Germany. The first French daily newspaper, *Le Journal de Paris,* did not appear until 1777. The first German daily had appeared more than a century earlier, in Leipzig in 1660. Yet a substantial reading public had existed in France since the seventeenth century, and it expanded

enormously in the eighteenth century, especially in cities and in
northern France, where nearly half of all adult males could read by
1789. This public was curious about public affairs and conscious of
itself as a new force in politics—that is, as public opinion—even
though it had no voice in the conduct of the government.[11]

So a basic contradiction existed: between the public with its
hunger for news on the one side and the state with its absolutist
forms of power on the other. To understand how this contradiction
played itself out, we need to take a closer look at the media that
transmitted news and the messages they conveyed. What were the
media in eighteenth-century Paris?

WE TEND to think of them by way of contrast with the all-
pervasive media of today. So we imagine the Old Regime as a simple, tranquil, media-free world-we-have-lost, a society with no
telephones, no television, no E-mail, Internet, and all the rest. In
fact, however, it was not a simple world at all. It was merely different. It had a dense communication network made up of media and
genres that have been forgotten, so thoroughly forgotten that even
their names are unknown today and cannot be translated into English equivalents: *mauvais propos, bruit public, on-dit, pasquinade,
pont-neuf, canard, feuille volante, factum, libelle, chronique scandaleuse.*
There were so many modes of communication, and they intersected and overlapped so intensively that we can hardly picture
their operation. I have tried to make a picture, nonetheless, a
schematic diagram that illustrates how messages traveled through
different media and milieus. (See Figure 5.)

Now, this model may look so complicated as to be absurd, more
like a diagram for wiring a radio than the flow of information
through a social system. Instead of elaborating on it, let me provide
an example of the transmission process, something you might liken

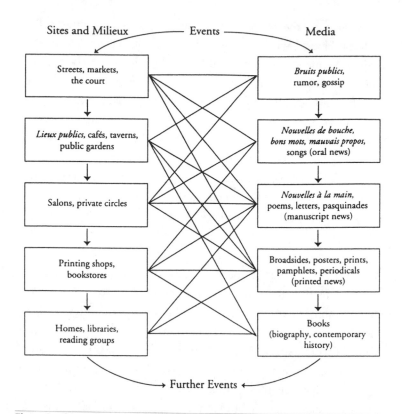

Sites and Milieux —— Events —— Media

Streets, markets, the court	*Bruits publics,* rumor, gossip
Lieux publics, cafés, taverns, public gardens	*Nouvelles de bouche, bons mots, mauvais propos,* songs (oral news)
Salons, private circles	*Nouvelles à la main,* poems, letters, pasquinades (manuscript news)
Printing shops, bookstores	Broadsides, posters, prints, pamphlets, periodicals (printed news)
Homes, libraries, reading groups	Books (biography, contemporary history)

→ Further Events ←

Fig. 5. A schematic model of a communication circuit. From Robert Darnton, *The Forbidden Best-Sellers of Pre-Revolutionary France* **(New York, 1995), 189.**

to a modern news flash. I quote from *Anecdotes sur Mme. la comtesse du Barry,* a top best seller on the eve of the French Revolution (about which more later):

We find in the manuscript gazette that has often guided us in assembling the materials for our history, an anecdote [about Mme. du Barry] that illustrates the general opinion of the public about her dominance of the king. It is dated March 20, 1773: "There is a report, carefully spread about by some courtiers, which proves that Mme. du Barry has not lost any favor or familiarity with the king, as some had suspected. His Majesty likes to brew his own coffee and, by means of this innocent amusement, to get some relief from the heavy burdens of government. A few days ago, the coffeepot began to boil over while His Majesty was distracted by something else. 'Hey France!' called out the beautiful favorite. 'Look out! Your coffee's buggering off.' [*La France, ton café fout le camp.*] We are told that 'France' is the familiar expression utilized by this lady in the intimacy of the king's private chambers [*petits apartements*]. Such details should never circulate outside of them, but they escape, nonetheless, thanks to the malignity of the courtiers."[12]

The anecdote is trivial in itself, but it illustrates the way a news item moved through various media, reaching an ever-wider public. In this case, it went through four phases: First, it began as *mauvais propos,* or insider gossip at court. Second, it turned into a *bruit public,* or general rumor in Paris, and the text uses a strong expression: "the general opinion of the public." Third, it became incorporated in *nouvelles à la main,* or manuscript news sheets, which circulated in the provinces, like Mme. Doublet's. Fourth, it was printed in a *libelle,* or scandalous book—in this case, a best seller, which went through many editions and reached readers everywhere.

The book, *Anecdotes sur Mme. la comtesse du Barry,* is a scurrilous biography of the royal mistress pieced together from bits of gossip picked up by the greatest *nouvelliste* of the century, Mathieu-François Pidansat de Mairobert. He went around Paris collecting tidbits of news and scribbling them on scraps of paper, which he stuffed into his pockets and sleeves. When he arrived in a café, he would pull one out and regale the company—or trade it for another item collected by another *nouvelliste.* Mairobert's biography of du Barry is really a scrapbook of these news items strung together along a narrative line, which takes the heroine from her obscure birth as the daughter of a cook and a wandering friar to a star role in a Parisian whorehouse and finally the royal bed.[13]

Mairobert did not hesitate to vent his political opinions in telling his story, and his opinions were extremely hostile to Versailles. In 1749 a police spy reported that he had denounced the government in the following terms: "Speaking about the recent reorganization of the army, Mairobert said in the Café Procope that any soldier who had an opportunity should blast the court to hell, since its sole pleasure is in devouring the people and committing injustices."[14] A few days later the police hauled him off to the Bastille, his pockets bulging with poems about taxes and the sex life of the king.

Mairobert's case, and dozens like it, illustrate a point so self-evident that it has never been noticed: The media of the Old Regime were mixed. They transmitted an amalgam of overlapping, interpenetrating messages, spoken, written, printed, pictured, and sung. The most difficult ingredient in this mixture for the historian to isolate and analyze is oral communication, because it usually disappeared into the air. But evanescent as it was, contemporaries took it seriously. (See Figure 6.) They often remarked on it in letters and diaries, and some of their comments conform quite closely to the model that I just presented in the form of a flow chart. Here, for example, is a contemporary description of how news traveled by word of mouth: "A vile courtier puts these infamies [reports of royal orgies] into rhyming couplets and, through the intermediary of flunkies, distributes them all the way to the marketplace. From the markets they reach artisans, who in turn transmit them back to the noblemen who first wrought them and who, without wasting a minute, go to the royal chambers in Versailles and whisper from ear to ear in a tone of consummate hypocrisy, 'Have you read them? Here they are. This is what is circulating among the common people in Paris.'"[15]

Fortunately for the historian, if not for the French, the Old Regime was a police state—"police" being understood in the eighteenth-century manner as municipal administration—and the police appreciated the importance of public opinion. They kept track of it by posting spies wherever people gathered to discuss public affairs—in marketplaces, shops, public gardens, taverns, and cafés. Of course spy reports and police files should not be taken literally. They have built-in biases, which sometimes reveal more about the police themselves than the persons they were observing. But if handled with care, the archives of the police provide enough information for one to see how oral networks functioned. I should like to draw on them in order to discuss two modes of communication that operated most effectively in eighteenth-century Paris: gossip and songs.

FIRST, GOSSIP. The papers of the Bastille are full of cases like Mairobert's: people arrested for *mauvais propos,* or insolent talk about public figures, especially the king. The sample is biased, of course, because the police did not arrest people who spoke favorably of Versailles, and a similar slant may distort the other principal source, spy reports, which sometimes concentrated on irreligion and sedition. Usually, however, the spies recounted casual discussions about all sorts of subjects among ordinary Parisians, and during the early years of Louis XV's reign the talk sounded favorable to the monarchy. I have studied reports on 179 conversations in 29 cafés between 1726 and 1729. (For a list, see Figure 7.) The sample is far from complete, because Paris had about 380 cafés at that time, but it indicates the topics and the tone of the talk in cafés located along the most important channels of communication, as one can see from the map in Figure 8. (For extensive excerpts from

the spy reports and a detailed mapping of the cafés on segments of the Plan Turgot, see the Web version of this chapter.)[16]

Most of the reports were written in dialogue. Here is an example:

At the Café de Foy someone said that the king had taken a mistress, that she was named Gontaut, and that she was a beautiful woman, the

Fig. 6. Conversation in a café.
Courtesy of the BNF, 67B 41693.
Here is an excerpt from "Mapping
Café Talk" (a supplementary study
that accompanies the electronic version of this essay is available at www.
historycooperative.org/ahr): *Café de
Foy, Palais-Royal.* "Some said that
they had heard the Controller General [Le Peletier de Forts, appointed
on June 15, 1726, at the time of the
revaluation of the currency] was
teetering and might fall. Others
said, 'Come on, that's nothing more
than what you hear in the current
songs. It looks very unlikely; and if
he left the government, the cardinal
[André-Hercule de Fleury, the dominant figure in the government by
June 1726] would leave also. It's
nothing more than a false alarm.'"

niece of the duc de Noailles and the comtesse de Toulouse. Others
said, "If so, then there could be some big changes." And another
replied, "True, a rumor is spreading, but I find it hard to believe, since
the cardinal de Fleury is in charge. I don't think the king has any incli-
nation in that direction, because he has always been kept away from
women." "Nevertheless," someone else said, "it wouldn't be the great-

Fig. 7. List of the twenty-nine cafés.

1. Coton, rue Saint-Denis: 29 reports
2. Foy, Palais-Royal: 28 reports
3. Rousseau, rue Saint-Antoine: 27 reports
4. Veuve Joseph, Pont Notre Dame: 9 reports
5. Feret, butte Saint-Roche: 7 reports
6. Gradot, quai de l'École: 7 reports
7. Dupuy, rue Saint-Honoré, près les Quinze-Vingts (?): 7 reports
8. Au prophète Élie, rue Saint-Honoré, au coin de la rue du Four: 6 reports
9. Conti, Pont-Neuf, au coin de la rue Dauphine: 6 reports
10. Paul, rue des mauvaises-Paroles, contre la Grande Poste: 5 reports
11. Marchand, quai Pelletier: 5 reports
12. Régence, rue Saint-Honoré, Place du Palais-Royal: 5 reports
13. Poncelet, quai de l'École: 4 reports
14. Moisy, rue Saint-Séverin: 4 reports
15. Veuve Laurent, rue Dauphine, au coin de la rue Christine: 4 reports
16. Baptiste, rue Dauphine: 4 reports
17. Ferré, Pont Saint-Michel: 3 reports
18. La Haude, rue Saint-Martin: 3 reports
19. Lescures, près de la Comédie: 3 reports
20. Marion, derrière la Barrière des Sergents: 2 reports
21. Bourbon, rue Bourtibourg: 2 reports
22. Procope, rue de la Comédie: 2 reports
23. Clorjean, rue royale Saint-Antoine: 1 report
24. Grignon, au coin de la rue Jean Saint-Denis: 1 report
25. La Perelle, rue Saint-Honoré: 1 report
26. Maugis, rue Saint-Séverin: 1 report
27. Gantois, rue Mazarine: 1 report
28. Le Roy, rue des Arts: 1 report
29. Duture, rue Dauphine: 1 report

est evil if he had a mistress." "Well, messieurs," another added, "it may not be a passing fancy, either, and a first love could raise some danger on the sexual side and could cause more harm than good. It would be far more desirable if he liked hunting better than that kind of thing."[17]

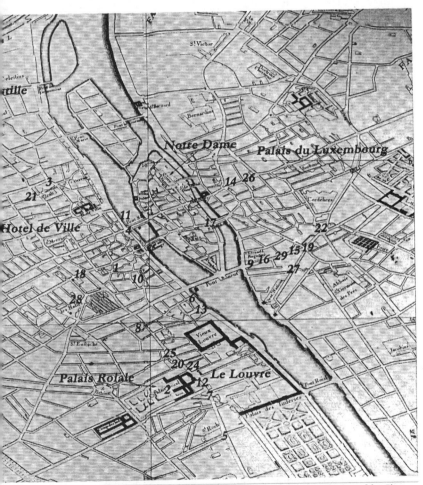

Fig. 8. Map of Paris with cafés indicated by number. Map designed by Jian Liu and researched by Sean Quinlan.

As always, the royal sex life provided prime material for gossip, but the reports all indicate that the talk was friendly. In 1729, when the queen was about to give birth, the cafés rang with jubilation: "Truly, everyone is delighted, because they all hope greatly to have a dauphin. . . . In the Café Dupuy, someone said, 'Parbleu, messieurs, if God graces us with a dauphin, you will see Paris and the whole river aflame [with fireworks in celebration].' Everyone is praying for that."[18] On September 4 the queen did indeed produce a dauphin, and the Parisians went wild with joy, not merely to have an heir to the throne but also to have the king in their midst, for Louis celebrated the birth with a grand feast in the Hotel de Ville following the fireworks. Royal magnificence choreographed to perfection in the heart of the city: That was what Parisians wanted from their king, according to the spy reports: "One of them said [in the Café de Foy], 'Parbleu, messieurs, you could never see anything more beautiful than Paris yesterday evening, when the king made his joyful entry into the Hôtel de Ville, speaking to everyone with the greatest affability, dining to a concert by two dozen musicians; and they say the meal was of the utmost magnificence.'"[19]

Twenty years later the tone had changed completely:

In the shop of the wigmaker Gaujoux, this individual [Jules-Alexis Bernard] read aloud in the presence of Sieur Dazemar, an invalid officer, an attack on the king in which it was said that His Majesty let himself be governed by ignorant and incompetent ministers and had made a shameful, dishonorable peace [the Treaty of Aix-la-Chapelle], which gave up all the fortresses that had been captured . . . ; that the king, by his affair with the three sisters, scandalized his people and would bring down all sorts of misfortune on himself if he did not change his conduct; that His Majesty scorned the queen and was an adulterer; that he had not confessed for Easter communion and would bring down the curse of God upon the kingdom and that France would be overwhelmed with disasters; that the duc de Richelieu was a pimp, who would crush Mme. de Pompadour or be crushed by her. He promised to show Sieur Dazemar this book, entitled *The Three Sisters*.[20]

What had happened between those two dates, 1729 and 1749? A great deal, of course: a flare-up of the Jansenist religious controversy, a running battle between the parlements and the crown, a major war, some disastrous harvests, and the imposition of unpopular taxes. But I should like to stress another factor, the end of the royal touch.

LET ME TELL YOU A STORY. Call it "The Three Sisters." Once upon a time, there was a nobleman, the marquis de Nesle, who had three daughters, one more beautiful than the other—or, if not exactly beautiful, at least ready and eager for sexual adventure. But that is a delicate subject, so I had better disguise their names and set the story in Africa.

So: Once upon a time, in the African kingdom of the Kofirans, a young monarch, Zeokinizul, began to eye the ladies in his court. (If you choose to unscramble the names—Kofirans/Français, Zeokinizul/Louis Quinze—that is up to you.) The king was a timid soul, interested in nothing except sex, and he was pretty timid at that too. But the first sister, Mme. de Liamil (Mailly) overcame his awkwardness and dragged him to bed. She had been coached by the chief minister, a mullah (prelate) named Jeflur (Fleury), who used her influence to fortify his own. But then the second sister, Mme. de Leutinemil (Vintimille), decided to play the same game, and she succeeded even better, thanks to tutoring from a still more wicked courtier, the kam de Kelirieu (duc de Richelieu). She died, however, after giving birth to a child.

So the king took up the third sister, Mme. de Lenertoula (La Tournelle, later the duchesse de Châteauroux), the most beautiful and ambitious of them all. She too accepted counsel from the wicked Kelirieu, and she conquered the king so completely that soon she was ruling the kingdom. Blinded by passion, Zeokinizul took her with him to the front when he set off to repulse an invasion of the Maregins (Germans). His subjects grumbled that kings should leave their mistresses at home when they did battle. In fact the attempt to make love as well as war proved to be more than Zeokinizul's constitution could bear. He fell ill, so deathly ill, that the doctors gave him up for lost, and the mullahs prepared to give him the last rites. But it looked as though the king might die unshriven, because Mme. de Lenertoula and Kelirieu refused to allow anyone else near the royal bedside. Finally, one mullah broke into the bedroom. He warned Zeokinizul of the danger of damnation. As the price for administering confession and extreme unction, he demanded that the king renounce his mistress. Lenertoula departed under a volley of insults, the king received the sacraments, and then—miracle!—he recovered.

His people rejoiced. His enemies retreated. He returned to his palace . . . and began to think it over. The mullah had been awfully insistent about hellfire. Mme. de Lenertoula was awfully beautiful. . . . So the king called her back. And then she promptly died. End of story.

What is the moral of this tale? For Parisians, it meant that the king's sins would bring down the punishment of God, and everyone would suffer, as Bernard proclaimed during the discussion of *The Three Sisters,* the version of the story that he declaimed in the shop of the wigmaker Gaujoux.

For historians, the story can be taken as a symptom of a rupture in the moral ties that bound the king to his people. After the death of Mme. de Châteauroux on December 8, 1744, Louis never again set foot in Paris, except for a few unavoidable ceremonies. In 1750 he built a road around the city so that he could travel from Versailles to Compiègne without exposing himself to the Parisians. He had also ceased to touch the sick who lined up in the Great Gallery of the Louvre in order to be cured of the King's Evil, or scrofula. This breakdown in ritual signaled the end—or at least the beginning of the end—of the *roi-mage,* the sacred, thaumaturgic king known to us through the work of Marc Bloch. By mid-century Louis XV had lost touch with his people, and he had lost the royal touch.[21]

That conclusion, I admit, is much too dramatic. Desacralization or delegitimation was a complex process, which did not occur all at once but rather by fits and starts over a long time span. In recounting this tale about Louis's love life, I did not mean to argue that he suddenly lost his legitimacy in 1744, although I believe he badly damaged it. My purpose was to suggest the way stories struck the consciousness of Parisians by the middle of the century.

To modern Americans, the story of the three sisters may read like an unconvincing blend of folklore and soap opera. But to eighteenth-century Parisians, it served as a gloss on current events: Louis XV's brush with death at Metz in August 1744, the disgrace of Mme. de Châteauroux, the general rejoicing at the king's recovery, and the general consternation at his decision to recall his mistress. The story also conveyed a prophecy of doom. Louis XV had compounded adultery with incest because fornicating with sisters had an incestuous character in eighteenth-century eyes. Thus the report of a spy who warned the police about the public's consternation at the king's affair with Mme. de Châteauroux in 1744: "Businessmen, retired officers, the common people are all complaining, speaking ill of the government and predicting that this war will have disastrous consequences. Clergymen, especially the Jansenists, take that view and dare to think and to say aloud that the evils that will soon overwhelm the kingdom come from above, as punishment for the incest and irreligion of the king. They cite passages from Scripture, which they apply [to the present circum-

stances]. The government should pay attention to this class of subjects. They are dangerous."[22]

Sin on such a scale would call down punishment from heaven,
not merely on the king but on the entire kingdom. Having been
anointed with the holy oil preserved since the conversion of Clovis
in the Cathedral of Reims, Louis XV had sacred power. He could
cure subjects afflicted with scrofula simply by touching them. After
his coronation in 1722 he had touched more than two thousand,
and he continued to touch the diseased for the next seventeen
years, particularly after taking communion on Easter. In order to
exercise that power, however, he had to cleanse himself from sin by
confession and communion. But his confessors would not admit
him to the Eucharist unless he renounced his mistresses, and he
refused to renounce them after 1738, when he began openly to
exhibit his adultery with Mme. de Mailly. From that time on, Louis
never again took Easter Communion and never again touched the
sick. The Metz crisis revived hope that he would recover his spiritual potency, but its denouement, the death of Mme. de Châteauroux and the succession of mistresses that began with the
installation of Mme. de Pompadour in 1745, signaled the end of
Louis's effectiveness as a mediator between his people and their
angry God. That was the conclusion reached by Bernard after
declaiming *The Three Sisters* to his audience in the wigmaker's shop.

At this point I should pause to deal with an objection. You may
concede that the police reports provide evidence about the public's
fear of divine retribution for the king's sins, but you also might
protest that my version of "The Three Sisters" does not necessarily
coincide with the story recounted in the 1740s by Parisians. Perhaps in a fit of postmodern permissiveness, I simply made it up.

I did not. Like many others, I deplore the current tendency to
mix fiction with fact, and I disagree with those who take liberties
with evidence on the ground that history requires unavoidable

doses of tropes.[23] I therefore looked far and wide for a book titled *Les Trois Soeurs*. I failed to find it, but I did come up with four other books published between 1745 and 1750 that tell the story of Louis's love affairs. They are all *romans à clef*, or novels in which real persons appear as fictitious characters. The story may be set in Africa (*Les Amours de Zeokinizul, roi des Kofirans*, 1747), Asia (*Mémoires secrets pour servir à l'histoire de Perse*, 1745), fairyland (*Tanastès, conte allégorique*, 1745), or an exotic island (*Voyage à Amatonthe*, 1750). But they all read like a commentary on current events, and they all condemn the king. The story of "The Three Sisters" as I recounted it is a faithful synopsis of *Les Amours de Zeokinizul,* and it fits the narrative line of all the others.[24]

The meaning of those novels for their readers can be ascertained with some accuracy because they all have keys. A collection of keys is available in the Bibliothèque de l'Arsenal, ms. 7067, and many of the copies of the novels have keys printed at the end, entered in handwriting, or inserted in the binding. (See Figure 9.) Decoding with a key, however, turns out to be a less mechanistic process than you might expect. If you work through a novel with a key in hand, you find yourself reading simultaneously at different levels and reading between the lines. A stilted story can come alive, once it is found to conceal another, naughtier story, and the inside stories proliferate as you penetrate deeper and deeper into the text. Some references are obvious, but others are ambiguous, and some are unexplained. In fact the keys occasionally contradict one another or contain manuscript corrections. So reading with a key becomes a kind of puzzle solving, and the heart of the mystery turns out in the end to be *le secret du roi,* the private life of the king, which is the ultimate mainspring of power. The *Vie privée de Louis XV,* a best-selling *libelle* of the 1780s, incorporated all this literature from the 1740s, often word for word, in a four-volume history of the entire reign.

Sophisticated literature of this sort might seem to be far

Kisinare	Marquise.
Kosir	Paris.
Kosirans	François.
Kransf	Francs.
Krinelbol	Crebillon.

L

Lenertoula	la Tournelle.
Leosanil	Noailles.
Leutinemil	Ventimille.
Liamil	Mailli.
Liegnelau	l'Evangile.
Lundamberk (*Kam*	le Duc de Cumber-
de) . . .	land.

M

Manoris	Romains.
Maregins	Germains *ou* Alle-
	mands.
Meani (*Kam de*) . .	le Duc du Maine.

N

Neitilane	Italienne.
Nbir	le Rhin.
Nodais	Danois.

O

Omeriserufs	Sou-Fermiers.
Ourtavan	Vantadour.

P

Pemenralt	Parlement.
Pepa	Pape.

R

Reinarol	Lorraine.

S

Sesems	Messes.
Sicidem	Medicis.
Sokans	Saxons.

Suß	Jesus.

T

Tesoulou	Toulouse.
Tueska	l'Escaut.

V

Vameric	Maurice Comte de Saxe.
Visir (un)	Mr. de Maurepas.
Vorompdap	Pompadour.
Vosaie	Savoie.

Z

Zeokinizul	Louis quinze.
Zeoteirizul	Louis treize.
Zekitaresoul	Louis quatorze.

le traducteur (crébillon) s'est trompé, si on en croit une méchante histoire de la favorite qui vient de paroître. Vorompdap est demeurée fidèle au Roi, lequel a récompensé son amour par sa constance; son époux vit voluptueusement dans un palais magnifique éloigné seulement de quelques lieues de Kosir [la gazette dit qu'en 1764 il acheta les prémices de la célèbre Vosaie], jeune merveille de l'Opéra qui fait depuis long-tems les délices du public. Peut etre qu'il y avoit une lacune dans le manuscrit, notre auteur les aime, car il a bien dit du mal des femmes: on sait d'ailleurs que les orphelins lui reprochent qu'il ne fait pas bien ses ouvrages. ah! quel conte!

Fig. 9. Part of a key to the anagrams in *Les Amours de Zeokinizul, roi des Kofirans: Ouvrage traduit de l'Arabe du voyageur Krinelbol* (Amsterdam, 1746), attributed to Laurent Angliviel de La Beaumelle and to Claude-Prosper Jolyot de Crébillon, fils. Photo courtesy of the Department of Rare Books and Special Collections, Princeton University Library.

removed from the raw gossip that coursed through the cafés, but by 1750 these "public noises" conveyed the same themes: the ignominy of the king, the degradation of him by his mistresses, and the manipulation of the mistresses by vile courtiers. Consider a few examples taken from police reports on what Parisians were saying about Mme. de Pompadour in 1749:[25]

Le Bret: After running down Mme. de Pompadour by loose talk in various locales, he said that she had driven the king crazy by putting all sorts of notions in his head. The bitch is raising hell, he said, because

of some poems that attack her. Does she expect to be praised while she
is wallowing in crime?

Jean-Louis Le Clerc: Made the following remarks in the Café de Procope: That there never has been a worse king; that the court, the ministers and the Pompadour make the king do shameful things, which
utterly disgust his people.

François-Philippe Merlet: Accused of having said in the tennis court of
Veuve Gosseaume that Richelieu and the Pompadour were destroying
the reputation of the king; that he was not well regarded by his people, since he was driving them to ruin; and that he had better beware,
because the twentieth tax could cause some mischief to befall him.

Fleur de Montagne: Among other things, he said that the king's extravagant expenditures showed that he didn't give a f——— for his people;
that he knows they are destitute and yet he is piling on another tax, as
if to thank them for all the services they have rendered him. They must
be crazy in France, he added, to put up with. . . . He whispered the
rest into someone's ear.

The congruence of themes from the *mauvais propos* and the
libelles should not be surprising because talking and reading about
private lives and public affairs were inseparable activities. It was a
public reading of a *libelle* that touched off the seditious talk in the
wigmaker's shop. Moreover, "public noises" fed into the confection
of the texts. According to the police, the *Mémoires secrets pour servir
à l'histoire de Perse* was generated from the information gathered in
the circle of Mme. de Vieuxmaison, much as the *Mémoires secrets pour
servir à l'histoire de la République des Lettres en France* came out of
the salon of Mme. Doublet. Mme. de Vieuxmaison appears in the
police files as "small, very white, blond, with a perfidious physiog-
nomy. . . . She is very clever and being [also] very wicked, she
writes poems and couplets against everyone. . . . Her circle . . . is

the most dangerous in Paris and is strongly suspected of having produced the *Anecdotes de Perse*."[26]

The most remarkable example of talk translated into text was *Tanastès,* a *roman à clef* about the king and the three sisters by Marie-Madeleine-Joseph Bonafon, a twenty-eight-year-old chambermaid in Versailles. The police could not believe that a female domestic servant could compose such a work. Having traced it back to her, locked her into the Bastille, and summoned her for cross-examination, they found themselves faced with an enigma: A workingwoman author—could it be true? They kept returning to this question in the interrogations. Had Mlle. Bonafon really written books? they asked. Yes, she replied, and she named them: *Tanastès,* the beginning of another novel entitled *Le Baron de XXX,* several poems, and three unpublished plays. Baffled, the police continued questioning:

> Asked what it was that gave her a taste for writing? Hadn't she consulted someone who was familiar with the composition of books in order to learn how to go about organizing the ones she intended to write?
>
> Answered that she did not consult anyone; that since she reads a great deal, this had given her a desire to write; that she had imagined, moreover, that she could make a little money by writing. . . .
>
> Had she written the book out of her own imagination? Hadn't someone supplied her with written material to work over? Who was it that had given [that material] to her?
>
> Replied that no memoirs had been given to her, that she had composed her book by herself, that in fact she had fashioned it in her imagination. Agreed, however, that having her head full of what people were saying in public about what had happened during and after the king's illness, she had tried to make some use of it in her book.[27]

Once it began to circulate, the book—and especially the key, which was printed and sold separately—reinforced the "public

noises." From talk to print to talk, the process built on itself dialec-
tically, accumulating force and spreading ever wider. It is difficult
to follow, owing to the sparseness of evidence about oral exchanges
that occurred 250 years ago. But enough documentation has survived to suggest that by 1750 the talk of the town had turned deci-
sively against the king.

Now let's consider songs. They too were an important
medium for communicating news. Parisians commonly composed
verse about current events and set it to popular tunes such as "Malbrouck s'en va-t-en guerre" ("The Bear Went over the Mountain" in
America, "For He's a Jolly Good Fellow" in England). Songs served
as mnemonic devices. In a society that remained largely illiterate,
they provided a powerful means of transmitting messages, one that
probably functioned more effectively in eighteenth-century Paris
than commercial jingles do in America today. Parisians of all
stripes, from sophisticated salon lions to simple apprentices, shared
a common repertory of tunes, and anyone with a bit of wit could
improvise couplets, or the standard French ballad made up of
eight-syllable lines with interlocking rhymes, to melodies carried
in the head. As Louis-Sébastien Mercier remarked, "No event takes
place that is not duly registered in the form of a *vaudeville* [popular
song] by the irreverent populace."[28]

Some songs originated in the court, but they reached the common people, and the common people sang back. Artisans composed
songs and sang them at work, adding new verses to old tunes as the
occasion arose. Charles-Simon Favart, the greatest librettist of
the century, got his start as a boy by putting words to popular
melodies while rhythmically kneading the dough in his father's bak-
ery. He and his friends—Charles Collé, Pierre Gallet, Alexis Piron,
Charles-François Panard, Jean-Joseph Vadé, Toussaint-Gaspard
Taconnet, Nicolas Fromaget, Christophe-Barthélemy Fagan,

Gabriel-Charles Lattaignant, François-Augustin Paradis de Mon-crif—outdid one another at improvising bawdy ballads and drink-ing songs at first in Gallet's grocery store, later in the Café du Caveau. Their songs made the rounds of taverns, echoed in the streets, and found their way into popular theaters—at the Foire Saint-Germain, along the vaudeville shows of the boulevards, and ultimately in the Opéra-Comique. At a more plebeian level, ragged street singers, playing fiddles and hùrdy-gurdies, entertained crowds at the Pont-Neuf, the Quai des Augustins, and other strate-gic locations. Paris was suffused with songs. In fact, as the saying went, the entire kingdom could be described as "an absolute monarchy tempered by songs."[29]

In such an environment a catchy song could spread like wildfire, and as it spread, it grew—inevitably, because it acquired new phrasing in the course of oral transmission and because everyone could join in the game of grafting new stanzas onto the old. The new verses were scribbled on scraps of paper and traded in cafés just like the poems and anecdotes diffused by the *nouvellistes.* When the police frisked prisoners in the Bastille, they confiscated large quantities of this material, which can still be inspected in boxes at the Bibliothèque de l'Arsenal—tiny bits of paper covered with scribbling and carried about triumphantly, until the fatal moment when a police inspector, armed with a *lettre de cachet,* commanded, "Empty your pockets."[30] (See Figure 10.) A typical scrap of verse, the latest stanzas to "Qu'une bâtarde de catin" one of the most pop-ular songs attacking Mme. de Pompadour, the king, and court, was seized from the upper-left vest pocket of Pidansat de Mairobert during his interrogation in the Bastille.[31]

Mairobert lived like a literary hack—"rue des Cordeliers, at a laundrywoman's place on the third floor," according to his police dossier—and described himself as "without fortune, reduced to what he could provide by his talent."[32] But he frequented the ele-

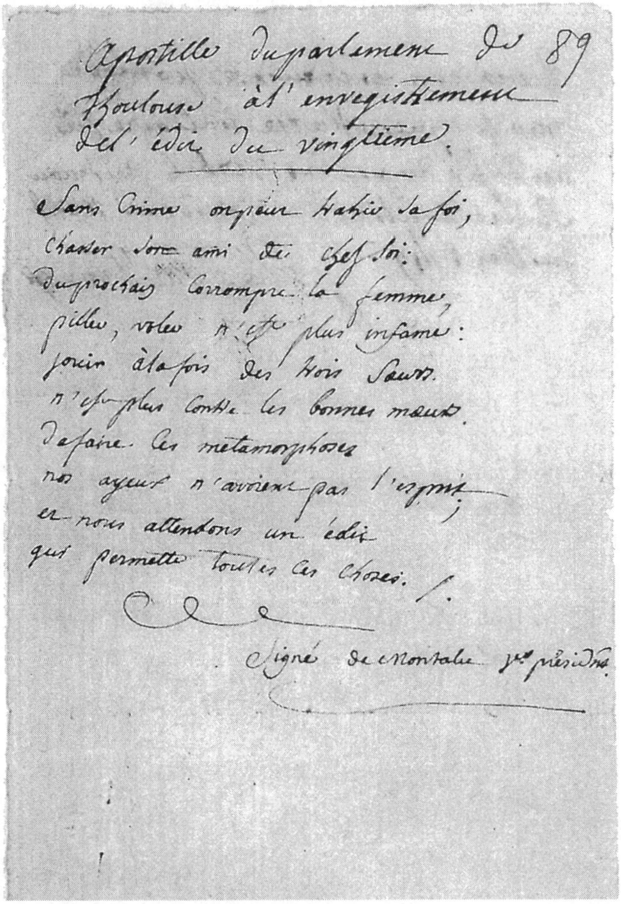
Apostille du parlement de Toulouse à l'enregistrement de l'édit du vingtième. 89

Sans Crime on peut trahir sa foi,
Chasser son ami de chez soi:
du prochain Corrompre la femme,
piller, voler n'est plus infame:
jouir à la fois des trois Soeurs.
n'est plus Contre les bonnes moeurs.
de faire ces metamorphoses
nos ayeux n'avoient pas l'esprit;
et nous attendons un édit
qui permette toutes ces Choses. /.

Signé de Montalu 1er président

Fig. 10. The police lifted this scrap of paper from a pocket of the abbé Guyard when they frisked him in the Bastille on July 10, 1749. The verse was dictated to Guyard by Pierre Sigorgne, a professor in the University of Paris, who had memorized a whole repertory of antigovernment songs and poems and declaimed them to his students. This poem, a burlesque edict by the Parlement of Toulouse, attacks the recent twentieth tax and various abuses of power, which it attributes to the immorality of the king as exemplified by his affair with the three daughters of the marquis de Nesle. Bibliothèque de l'Arsenal, ms. 11690, 1749.

gant company in Mme. Doublet's salon, and other song collectors belonged to the highest ranks of the court. The greatest of them all was the comte de Maurepas, minister of the navy and the king's household, one of the most powerful men in Versailles. Maurepas epitomized the court style of politics under Louis XV. Witty, canny, and unscrupulous, he covered his maneuvering with an air of gaiety that endeared him to the king. He also held on to Louis' favor by regaling him with the latest songs, even songs that made fun of Maurepas himself and especially those that ridiculed his rivals.[33]

This was a dangerous game, however, and it backfired. On April 24, 1749, the king dismissed Maurepas from the government and sent him into exile by *lettre de cachet*. Contemporaries interpreted Maurepas's fall as a spectacular upheaval in the power system of Versailles. What had caused it? they asked. The answer, as it appears in letters and diaries, was unanimous: not political conflict, not ideological opposition, not questions of principle or policy or even patronage . . . but songs, and one song, in particular, written to the tune "Quand le péril est agréable":[34]

> *Par vos façons nobles et franches,*
> *Iris, vous enchantez nos coeurs;*
> *Sur nos pas vous semez des fleurs.*
> *Mais ce sont des fleurs blanches.*

To the modern reader, the text, and the entire episode, are utterly opaque. Translated literally, the song sounds like an innocent exercise in gallantry:

> By your noble and free manner,
> Iris, you enchant our hearts.
> On our path you strew flowers.
> But they are white flowers.

To insiders in Versailles, however, the meaning was obvious, and it showed that the current wave of songs had gone beyond the boundaries of the permissible, even among the nastiest wits at court. The song cast Pompadour as Iris (some versions referred to her by her ignoble maiden name, Poisson, or Fish) and alluded to an intimate dinner in the private chambers of the king, where Louis was supposed to be protected from gossip by a barrier of secrecy. The little party consisted of the king, Pompadour, Maurepas, and Pompadour's cousin Mme. d'Estrades. After arriving with a bouquet of white hyacinths, Pompadour distributed the flowers to her three companions: thus the "white flowers" in the song. But *fleurs blanches* also meant signs of venereal disease in menstrual discharge (*flueurs*).[25] Of the three witnesses, only Maurepas was capable of turning this episode into verse and leaking it to the court. So whether or not he had actually composed the song, it produced such outrage in the private chambers that he was stripped of power and banished from Versailles.

Of course there was much more to this than met the ear. Maurepas had enemies, notably his rival in the government, the comte d'Argenson, minister of war and an ally of Mme. de Pompadour's. Her position as *maîtresse en titre,* a quasi-official role designated by formal presentation at court, had not yet solidified to the point where she could consider herself invulnerable to gossip. A campaign of derision, orchestrated by Maurepas and conducted by means of songs, might persuade the king to renounce her in order to win back the respect of his subjects. Such at least was the opinion of some Parisians, who noted that the white flower song belonged to a flood of hostile verse that coursed through the city during the first six months of 1749.[36]

The tide did not turn after the fall of Maurepas—perhaps, according to some observers, because his partisans kept up the crescendo of songs after he had disappeared in order to prove that he had not been responsible for them in the first place. But whatever the tactics pursued at court, the singing in Paris caused the government serious concern. With the backing of the king, d'Argenson organized a campaign to wipe it out. He went into action as soon as he learned that Parisians had taken up a new song with the first line *"Monstre dont la noire furie"* (Monster whose black fury), the monster being Louis XV. From the ministry in Versailles to police headquarters in Paris, an order went out: Find the author of the verse that began with those words. The order passed down the chain of command from the lieutenant general of police to a squad of inspectors and spies. And before long Inspector Joseph d'Hémery received a note from an undercover agent: "I know someone who had a copy of the abominable verse against the king in his study a few days ago and who spoke approvingly of them. I can tell you who he is, if you want."[37] Just two sentences, without a signature, on a crumpled piece of paper, but they earned the spy twelve louis d'or, the equivalent of nearly a year's wages for an unskilled laborer, and they triggered an extraordinary poetry hunt and manhunt, which produced the richest dossiers of literary detective work that I have ever encountered. By following the police as they followed the poem, I shall try to reconstruct a network that shows how messages traveled through an oral communication system in eighteenth-century Paris.[38]

After a good deal of hugger-mugger, the police arrested the person who had possessed a handwritten text of the verse, a medical student named François Bonis. In his interrogation in the Bastille, he said he had got it from a priest, Jean Édouard, who was arrested and said he had got it from another priest, Inguimbert de Montange, who was arrested and said he had got it from a third priest, Alexis Dujast, who was arrested and said he had got it from a law student, Jacques-Marie Hallaire, who was arrested and said he had got it from a clerk in a notary's office, Denis-Louis Jouet, who was arrested . . . and so on down the line, until the trail gave out and the police gave up, fourteen arrests from the beginning. Each arrest generated its own dossier, and each dossier contains new evidence about the modes of communication. The overall pattern can be seen in the flow chart on the following page (Figure 11).

At first glance, the pattern looks straightforward, and the milieu seems to be homogeneous. The verse (poem 1 on the diagram) was passed along a line of students, priests, lawyers, notaries, and clerks, most of them friends and all of them young—between sixteen and thirty-one, generally in their early twenties. The verse itself gave off a corresponding odor, at least to the comte d'Argenson, who returned a copy to the lieutenant general of police with a note describing it as an "infamous piece, which seems to me, as to you, to smell of pedantry and the Latin Quarter."[39] But the picture became more complicated as the investigation broadened. When it reached Hallaire, the fifth person from the top of the diagram, the path of the poetry bifurcated. Hallaire had received three other poems from the abbé Guyard, who in turn had three further suppliers, who had suppliers of their own, and so on, until the police found themselves tracking a total of six poems and songs, one more seditious than the next (at least in the eyes of the authorities) and each with its own diffusion pattern.

In the end they filled the Bastille with fourteen purveyors of poetry, hence the name of the operation in the dossiers, "The Affair of the Fourteen." They never found the author of the original verse. In fact it may not have had an author at all, not because Roland Barthes and Michel Foucault have told us that the author is dead, but because people added and subtracted stanzas and modified phrasing as they pleased. It was a case of collective creation, and the first poem overlapped and intersected with so many others that taken together, they created a field of poetic impulses, bouncing from one transmission point to another and filling the air with *mauvais propos,* a cacophony of sedition set to rhyme.

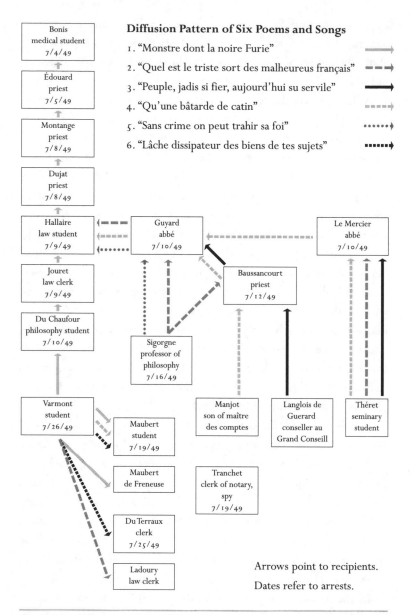

Diffusion Pattern of Six Poems and Songs

1. "Monstre dont la noire Furie"
2. "Quel est le triste sort des malheureus français"
3. "Peuple, jadis si fier, aujourd'hui su servile"
4. "Qu'une bâtarde de catin"
5. "Sans crime on peut trahir sa foi"
6. "Lâche dissipateur des biens de tes sujets"

Bonis
medical student
7/4/49

Édouard
priest
7/5/49

Montange
priest
7/8/49

Dujat
priest
7/8/49

Hallaire
law student
7/9/49

Guyard
abbé
7/10/49

Le Mercier
abbé
7/10/49

Jouret
law clerk
7/9/49

Baussancourt
priest
7/12/49

Du Chaufour
philosophy student
7/10/49

Sigorgne
professor of
philosophy
7/16/49

Varmont
student
7/26/49

Maubert
student
7/19/49

Manjot
son of maître
des comptes

Langlois de
Guerard
conseller au
Grand Conseill

Théret
seminary
student

Maubert
de Freneuse

Tranchet
clerk of notary,
spy
7/19/49

Du Terraux
clerk
7/25/49

Ladoury
law clerk

Arrows point to recipients.

Dates refer to arrests.

Fig. 11. The diffusion pattern of six poems and songs.

The interrogations of the suspects in the Bastille provide a picture of the settings in which the verse circulated as well as the modes of their transmission. At each point, the poetry readings were accompanied by discussion. Bonis said that he had copied the first poem in the Hôtel-Dieu, where he had found a friend deep in conversation with a priest. "The conversation turned on the subject matter of the gazettes; and this priest, saying that someone had been so wicked as to write some satirical verses about the king, pulled out a poem attacking His Majesty."[40] Hallaire testified that he had made his copy during a dinner with some friends in the house of his father, a silk merchant in the rue Saint-Denis. Montange copied the poem after hearing it read aloud during a bull session in the dining hall of his college. Pierre Sigorgne, a professor at the Collège du Plessis, dictated two of the poems to his students; it was a political *dictée* in the heart of the University of Paris! Sigorgne knew the poems by heart, and one of them had eighty-four lines. The art of memory was still flourishing in eighteenth-century Paris, and in several cases it was reinforced by the greatest mnemonic device of all, music, for some of the poems were composed to fit the rhythms of popular tunes, and they circulated by means of singing, along with the songs that came from the court and that had provoked the investigation in the first place.

Whether sung or declaimed from memory, the verse was copied on scraps of paper, which were carried about in pockets and swapped for other verses. The texts soon found their way into manuscript gazettes and, finally, into print. The two longest poems, "Quel est le triste sort des malheureux français" (What is the sad lot of the unhappy French) and "Peuple, jadis si fier, aujourd'hui si servile" (People, once so proud, today so servile), appeared prominently in *Vie privée de Louis XV,* the hostile history of the reign that became a best seller in the 1780s. In discussing the outburst of songs and poems in 1749, it observed:

It was at this shameful time that the general scorn for the sovereign and his mistress began to become manifest, then continued to grow until the end of the reign. . . . This scorn broke out for the first time in some satirical verse about the outrage committed to Prince Edward [Charles Edward Stuart, or Bonnie Prince Charlie, the Young Pretender, who was arrested in Paris on December 10, 1748, and expelled from the kingdom in accordance with the British demands accepted by France in the peace of Aix-la-Chapelle], where Louis XV is addressed in a passage that compares him with that illustrious exile:

> Il est roi dans les fers; qu'êtes-vous sur le trône?
> [He is a king in irons; what are you on the throne?]

And then, in an apostrophe to the nation:

> Peuple, jadis si fier, aujourd'hui si servile,
> Des princes malheureux vous n'êtes plus l'asile!

> [People, once so proud, today so servile,
> You no longer provide a sanctuary for unhappy princes!]

The eagerness of the public to seek out these pieces, to learn them by heart, to communicate them to one another, proved that the readers adopted the sentiments of the poet. Madame de Pompadour wasn't spared, either. . . . She ordered a drastic search for the authors, peddlers, and distributors of these pamphlets, and the Bastille was soon full of prisoners.[41]

In short, the communication process took place by several modes in many settings. It always involved discussion and sociability, so it was not simply a matter of messages transmitted down a line of diffusion to passive recipients but rather a process of assimilating and reworking information in groups—that is, the creation of collective consciousness or public opinion. If you will tolerate

some jargon, you could think of it as a multimedia feedback system. But that sounds rather fancy. I merely want to stress that there
are theoretical issues at stake in this kind of study and that in pursuing it, I have drawn on the sociology of communication developed by Elihu Katz and Gabriel Tarde rather than the more voguish
theories of Jürgen Habermas.[42]

But to return to the medium of singing, the song that circulated
most actively among the fourteen, "Qu'une bâtarde de catin," typ-
ified the ballads that had the most popular appeal in Paris. Its simple eight-syllable lines fitted a common tune, "Quand mon amant
me fait la cour," which was also identified in some sources as
"Dirai-je mon confiteor?" The *catin* (strumpet) in the first line was
Mme. de Pompadour. And the catchy refrain, *"Ah! le voilà, ah! le
voici / Celui qui n'en a nul souci,"* pointed a finger at the king, clue-
less, carefree Louis. The first verse went as follows:[43]

Qu'une bâtarde de catin
À la cour se voie avancée,
Que dans l'amour et dans le vin,
Louis cherche une gloire aisée,
Ah! le voilà, ah! le voici
Celui qui n'en a nul souci.

[That a bastard strumpet
Should get ahead in the court,
That in love and wine
Louis should seek some easy glory,
Ah! there he is, ah! there he is
He who doesn't have a care.]

Each verse satirized a public figure. After Pompadour and the
king, the song worked its way down through ministers, generals,

prelates, and courtiers. Everyone appeared incompetent or cor-rupt, and in each case the refrain reiterated the song's main theme: that the king, who should have taken responsibility for the welfare of his people, paid no heed to anything but drink and sex. While the kingdom went to hell, Louis remained "he who doesn't have a care." Although I cannot prove it, I think the song suggests a children's game—the kind in which one person stands in the middle of a cir-cle and the rest join hands and skip around him singing "the farmer in the dell" or "the cheese stands alone"—except here the singing is pure mockery: the king is the ultimate idiot.

The verses cover all the major events and political issues between 1748 and 1750, and the versification is so simple that new subjects of mockery could easily be added as events evolved. That is exactly what happened, as you can see by comparing all the surviv-ing versions of the song. I have found nine, scattered through vari-ous manuscript collections. They contain from six to twenty-three verses, the later ones alluding to the most recent events such as the notorious cuckolding of the tax farmer A.-J.-J. Le Riche de La Popelinière by the duc de Richelieu in the spring of 1750. Further-more, if you compare different versions of the same verse, you can find small differences in phrasing, which probably bear the mark of the oral diffusion process, since variations crept in as the song passed from one singer to another. The Parisians may not have been singers of tales, like the Serbs studied by Albert Lord, but they were singers of news.[44] "Qu'une bâtarde de catin" contained so much news and commentary that it can be considered a sung newspaper.

But it should not be considered in isolation, because it belonged to a vast corpus of songs, which extended nearly everywhere in Paris and covered virtually everything of interest to Parisians. It is impossible to measure the size of this corpus, but we can get some idea of its dimensions by examining all the evidence that remains in the archives. When consigned to writing, the songs first appeared on slips of paper like that in Figure 12, which contains a selection

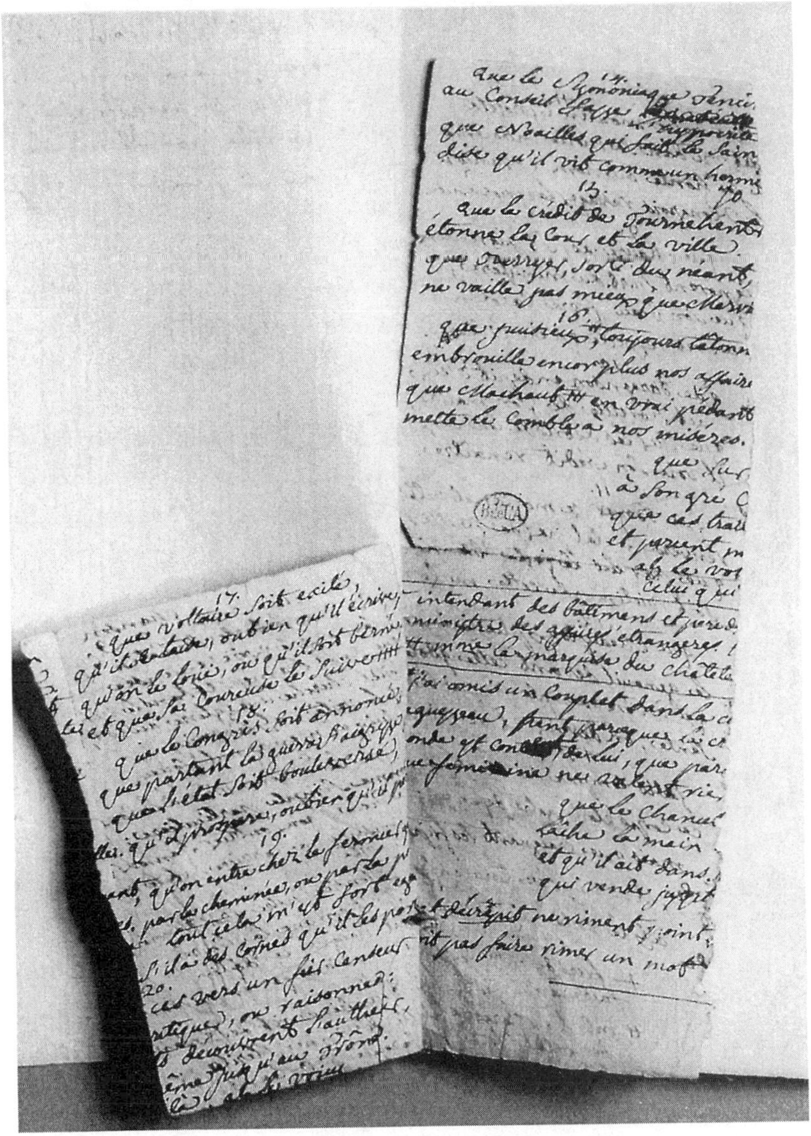

Fig. 12. Some verses from the song "Qu'une bâtarde de catin," taken from the abbé Guyard by the police when they searched him in the Bastille. Bibliothèque de l'Arsenal, ms. 11690, fols. 67–68, 1749.

of verses from "Qu'une bâtarde de catin" and came from a pocket of Christophe Guyard, one of the Fourteen, when he was frisked in the Bastille. As already explained, a similar scrap of paper, also with verses from "Qu'une bâtarde de catin," was confiscated from a pocket of Mairobert. He had no connection with the Fourteen, so he probably acquired the song by tapping into another network. Seven other copies, which have turned up in various libraries, probably came from still other sources. In short, the song had traveled through many channels of diffusion, and the network of the Fourteen was but a small segment of a very large whole.

How large? Consider the next category of evidence: collections. Many Parisians picked up scraps of paper scribbled with verse from cafés and public gardens, then stored them in their apartments. The police found sixty-eight of these snippets—songs, poems, scribbling of all sorts—when they searched Mairobert's room. Wealthier collectors had their secretaries transcribe this material into well-ordered registers, known as *chansonniers*. The most famous of these, the "Chansonnier Maurepas," contains Maurepas's own collection and runs to thirty-five volumes.[45] By studying it and seven other *chansonniers* from the mid-century years, I have formed a rough idea of how many songs existed at that time and which ones were the most popular. The richest source, a twelve-volume collection in the Bibliothèque historique de la Ville de Paris titled "Oeuvres diaboliques pour servir à l'histoire du temps," contains 641 songs and poems from the period 1745–1751 and 264 that date from the end of 1748 to the beginning of 1751.[46] It seems clear therefore that the six songs and poems exchanged among the Fourteen constituted only a tiny fraction of a gigantic repertory, but they show up everywhere in the *chansonniers,* along with a host of other songs and poems on the same subjects. "Qu'une bâtarde de catin" appears most often, eight times in all. It can be taken as a

fairly representative example of what Parisians sang in the middle
of the century.

A final run of documents makes it possible for us to have some
notion of what the Parisians heard. Of course the sounds themselves disappeared into the air 250 years ago, and they cannot be
duplicated exactly today. But a series of musical "keys," such as "La
Clef du Caveau" in the Bibliothèque nationale de France, contain
the actual music to the tunes cited in the *chansonniers*.[47] I am incapable of translating this manuscript into sound, but Hélène
Delavault, a gifted opera singer and cabaret performer from Paris,
kindly recorded fourteen of the songs for an electronic version of
this essay, which can be consulted on the Web at www.history
cooperative.org/ahr. All the songs concern current events from
1749, and two—the two I have just discussed, "Par vos façons
nobles et franches" and "Qu'une bâtarde de catin"—come directly
out of the Affair of the Fourteen. As the Web concert demonstrates,
modern information technology can open up new access to the age
of information in the eighteenth century. It can make history sing.

INSTEAD OF CHASING gossip and songs farther down the channels
of oral communication, I should like to turn the argument in a different direction, one that leads toward the French Revolution. That
territory, the most embattled in all historical studies, is mined with
conceptual difficulties. In order to clear a way through it, I would
suggest three propositions about the history of communication in
general.

First, it makes no sense, I think, to separate printed from oral
and written modes of communication, as we casually do when we
speak of print culture, because they all were bound together in a
multimedia system. Nor, second, does it serve any purpose to
derive one mode of communication from another, as if our task,

like that of the police, were to trace a message to its source. It was the spread of the message that mattered—not its origin but its amplification, the way it reached the public and ultimately took hold. That process should be understood as a matter of feedback and convergence, rather than one of trickling down and linear causality. Third, it is equally misleading to distinguish separate realms of popular and elite culture. Despite the stratified character of Parisian society under the Old Regime, its publics crossed paths and rubbed elbows everywhere. They were mixed. In studying communication, I recommend that we look for mixtures, of milieus as well as media.

Having delivered myself of those imperatives, I realize that I am still far from having proved my argument. Until now I have merely described what news was and the way it was transmitted, not how people made sense of it. That last step is the most difficult because it has to do with reception as well as diffusion. We have plenty of reception theory but very little evidence about how reception actually took place. I cannot come up with a solution to that problem, but I may have found a detour that will help us get around it.

Let's consider once more the "news flash" about Louis XV's coffee spilling. How can we know what eighteenth-century readers made of it? We have no record of their reactions. But we can study the way the text works, the manner in which it fits into the book, *Anecdotes sur Mme. la comtesse du Barry;* and the book's place in a corpus of related texts, which provided the basic fund of information about current events and contemporary history to the general reading public.

I would begin with the key phrase *La France! Ton café fout le camp.* It would have sounded particularly shocking to eighteenth-century ears, because *La France* evoked a particular meaning in the social code of the time. Lackeys were often called by the province of their origin. So by shouting out "La France" in an unguarded moment, du Barry was calling the king her lackey.[48] She did so in a spectacularly vulgar manner, one that could be taken to reveal the plebeian nature

beneath her courtly veneer, for *fout le camp* was the language of the
brothel, not the court. Similar outbursts of vulgarity occur throughout the book. In fact they constitute its central theme. *Anecdotes sur
Mme. la comtesse du Barry* was a classic *libelle,* organized according to
the formula that I mentioned earlier: from the brothel to the throne.
Du Barry sleeps her way to the top, using tricks she picked up in the
whorehouse to revive the exhausted libido of the old king and thus
to dominate the kingdom. She is a sluttish Cinderella and therefore
different from all previous royal mistresses—or all since Mme. de
Pompadour, née Poisson—who, whatever their morals, were at
least ladies. This theme is summed up by a song, one of many songs
printed in the book, which includes the lines:

> *Tous nos laquais l'avaient eue,*
> *Lorsque traînant dans la rue,*
> *Vingt sols offerts à sa vue*
> *La déterminaient d'abord.*

> [All our lackeys had her
> In the days when she walked the streets,
> And twenty sols offered up front
> Made her accept at once.][49]

The rhetoric plays on the assumption that readers wanted their
kings to be discriminating in their gallantry, just as they were
expected to be heroic in war, regal in court, and pious in church.
Louis XV failed on all counts, although he got high marks for his
bravery at the Battle of Fontenoy in 1745. He was the antithesis of
France's favorite king, Henri IV. And he was reviled in the book, not
because the author held him up to any radical or republican standard of statecraft but because he had not been kingly enough. Thus
a second leitmotif that runs throughout the text, the degradation of
the monarchy. At every point the narrative dwells on the profana-

tion of royal symbols and the person of the king himself. The scepter, it says, has become as feeble as the royal penis.[50]

This was strong language for an age that treated kings as sacred beings directly ordained to rule by God and invested with the royal touch. But Louis had lost his touch, as I explained earlier. *Anecdotes sur Mme. la comtesse du Barry* compounded that loss by presenting him as an ordinary mortal—or, worse, as a dirty old man. At the same time, it invited the reader to enjoy the *frisson* of seeing into the innermost chambers of Versailles, into the *secret du roi* itself, even to observe the king between the sheets. For that is where the great affairs of state were decided: the fall of Choiseul, the partition of Poland, the destruction of France's judicial system by the chancellor Maupeou, everything that would have warranted a banner headline, if there had been headlines, or newspapers with news. In each case, as the story went, du Barry filled the king with drink, dragged him to bed, and got him to sign any edict that had been prepared for her by her evil counselors. This kind of reportage anticipated techniques that would be developed a century later in yellow journalism: It presented the inside story of politics in Versailles; it pictured power struggles as what the butler saw; it reduced complex affairs of state to backstairs intrigue and the royal sex life.

That of course was hardly serious history. I would call it folklore. But it had enormous appeal, so much that it is still alive today. I found the coffee-spilling episode—with the wrong mistress but the right emphasis on her vulgarity—in a French-Canadian comic book. (See Figure 13.) Instead of dismissing political folklore as trivial, I would take it seriously. In fact I believe it was a crucial ingredient in the collapse of the Old Regime. But before leaping to that conclusion, I had better retreat to familiar territory, the trade in forbidden books, which I studied in my last round of research. The main results of this study can be summarized in the following best seller list, which shows which books circulated most widely in

Fig. 13. The coffee-spilling episode as pictured in a modern-day French-Canadian comic book. Mme. de Pompadour is mistakenly substituted for Mme. du Barry. From Léandre Bergeron and Robert Lavaill, *Petit manuel d'histoire de Québec* (n.p., n.d. [1970s]), 48.

the vast underground of illegal literature during the twenty years before the Revolution:[51]

L'An deux mille quatre cent quarante by L.-S. Mercier

Anecdotes sur Mme. la comtesse du Barry* by M.-F. Pidansat de Mairobert

Système de la nature by P.-H. baron d'Holbach

Tableau de Paris by L.-S. Mercier

Histoire philosophique by G.-T.-F. Raynal

*Journal historique de la révolution opérée . . . par M. de Maupeou** by M.-F.
     Pidansat de Mairobert and B.-J.-F. Moufle d'Angerville

L'Arrétin by H.-J. du Laurens

Lettre philosophique par M. de V——, anonymous

*Mémoires de l'abbé Terray** by J.-B.-L. Coquereau

La Pucelle d'Orléans by Voltaire

Questions sur l'Encyclopédie by Voltaire

*Mémoires de Louis XV,** anonymous

*L'Espion anglais** by M.-F. Pidansat de Mairobert

La Fille de joie, a translation of *Fanny Hill* by Fougeret de Montbrun (?)

Thérèse philosophe by J.-B. de Boyer, marquis d'Argens

Five of the top fifteen books on the list, those marked by asterisks, were *libelles* or *chroniques scandaleuses,* and there were dozens more. A huge corpus of scandalous literature reached readers everywhere in France, although it has been almost completely forgotten today—no doubt because it did not qualify as literature in the eyes of literary critics and librarians. The *libelles* often have impressive literary qualities, nonetheless. *Anecdotes sur Mme. la comtesse du Barry* made it to the top of the best seller list because, among other things, it was very well written. Mairobert knew how to tell a story. His text is funny, wicked, shocking, outrageous, and a very good read.

It also looks impressive physically. It comes packaged in an imposing, 346-page tome, complete with a handsome frontispiece and all the appearances of a serious biography. The other *libelles* are often more elaborate. They contain footnotes, appendices, genealogies, and all sorts of documentation. The *Vie privée de Louis XV* provides a four-volume history of the entire reign, more detailed and better documented—for all its scurrility—than many modern his-

tories. The *Journal historique de la révolution opérée . . . par M. de Maupeou* runs to seven volumes; *L'Espion anglais* runs to ten; *Mémoires
secrets pour servir à l'histoire de la République des Lettres en France* to
thirty-six.

These books charted the whole course of contemporary history.
In fact they were the only map available because political biography
and contemporary history—two genres that provide the backbone
of our own best seller lists—did not exist in the legal literature of
the Old Regime. They were forbidden.[52] Contemporaries who
wanted to orient themselves by relating the present to the recent
past had to turn to libel literature. They had nowhere else to go.

How did that process of orientation take place? If you read your
way through the entire corpus of *libelles* and *chroniques scandaleuses,*
you find the same traits, the same episodes, and often the same
phrases scattered everywhere. The authors drew on common
sources and lifted passages from one another's texts as freely as they
traded scraps of news in the cafés. It was not a matter of plagiarism,
because that notion hardly applied to underground literature, and
the books, like the songs, hardly had individual authors. It was a
case of rampant intertextuality.

Despite their baroque profusion, the texts can be reduced to a
few leitmotifs, which recur throughout the corpus: The court is
always sinking deeper into depravity, the ministers are always
deceiving the king, the king is always failing to fulfill his role as head
of state, the state's power is always being abused, and the common
people are always paying the price for the injustices inflicted on
them—higher taxes, increased suffering, more discontent, and
greater impotence in the face of an arbitrary and all-powerful government. Individual news items like the coffee spilling were stories
in themselves. But they also fitted into narrative frames of whole
books, and the books fitted into a metanarrative that ran through
the entire corpus: Politics was an endless series of variations on a
single theme, decadence and despotism.

True, I don't know how the readers read those books, but I don't think it extravagant to insist on a quality of reading in general; it is an activity that involves making sense of signs by fitting them in frames. Stories provide the most compelling frames. Ordinary people often find meaning in the booming, buzzing confusion of the world around them by telling, hearing, and reading stories. The general readers in eighteenth-century France made sense of politics by incorporating news into the narrative frames provided by the literature of libel. And they were reinforced in their interpretations by the messages they received from all the other media: gossip, poems, songs, prints, jokes, and all the rest.

I HAVE REACHED the end of my argument, and I realize that I have not proved it. To drive it home, I must push it in two directions. First, further back into the past. The corpus of *libelle* literature from the 1770s and 1780s grew out of an old tradition, which goes back beyond the Huguenot propaganda against Louis XIV, beyond the seditious libeling of Jules Mazarin (*mazarinades*), and beyond the pamphleteering of the religious wars to the art of insult and rumormongering developed in the Renaissance courts. From the political slander of Pietro Aretino onward, this tradition changed and grew, until it culminated in the vast outpouring of *libelles* under Louis XV and Louis XVI.53

Those *libelles* in turn provided a frame for the public's perception of events during the crisis of 1787–1788, which brought down the Old Regime. That is the second direction in which I would take the argument. But to explain how that happened, I shall have to write a book showing how the crisis was construed, day by day, in all the media of the time.

So I am issuing promissory notes instead of arriving at a firm conclusion. But I hope I have said enough to provoke some rethinking of the connections between the media and politics—even politics today. Although I am skeptical about attempts to make history teach lessons, I think that eighteenth-century Paris may provide some perspective on contemporary Washington. How do most Americans orient themselves amid political confusion and media blitzes? Not, I fear, by analyzing issues, but from our own variety of political folklore—that is, by telling stories about the private lives of our politicians, just as the French regaled themselves with the *Vie privée de Louis XV.* How can we make sense of it all? Not merely by reading our daily newspaper but by rereading the history of an earlier information age, when the king's secret was exposed beneath the Tree of Cracow and the media knitted themselves together in a communication system so powerful that it proved to be decisive in the collapse of the regime.

3

THE UNITY OF EUROPE:
CULTURE AND POLITENESS

THE INTRODUCTION OF THE EURO IN 2002 RAISED FUNDAMEN-
TAL QUESTIONS: WOULD THE CURRENCY UNIFY EUROPE? What
holds Europe together? How can Europe cohere as a community?

One thinks first of conquerors: Caesar, Charlemagne, Napoleon,
Hitler. But their empires crumbled, and the geography kept changing. Europe ended in the Germanic forests at one time and in the
Urals at another. It had no natural boundaries, not even in the West,
where the British still say they are setting off for Europe when they
drive their cars to France.

Europe is actually a state of mind. It began as a myth, the abduc-
tion of Europa, daughter of Agenor in Tyre, and it evolved into a way
of life based on the sense of belonging to a common civilization. This
mentalité collective developed through the civilizing process itself, the
shared experience of living under Roman law, Christian religion,
and the secular culture developed in the Age of Enlightenment.

That common culture fell apart in the nineteenth century, when
Europe broke up into nation-states, but its principles endured. Having been articulated by philosophers everywhere from Kant in
Königsberg to Filangieri in Naples, they were proclaimed in 1789 by
the Declaration of the Rights of Man and of the Citizen: "Men are
born and remain free and equal in rights. . . . These rights are liberty,

property, security, and resistance to oppression." They were reaffirmed by the Universal Declaration of the Rights of Man adopted by
the United Nations in 1948. They stand still as the foundation of the
Europe that has risen again at the end of the twentieth century.

Kissinger's famous *boutade*—"If I call Europe, what number do I
call?"—misses the point because Europe corresponds to a set of
symbols and a system of values. The euro is one of them, but its
value will fluctuate erratically, whereas the values of the Enlightenment are rooted deeply in the past.

Which past? Whose past? For the last two centuries Europe tore
itself in pieces; and it is still coming apart at the edges, in Ireland,
Russia, and the Balkans. Many things contributed to its dissolution,
industrial revolutions and class struggles among them. But the most
destructive force, the only one capable of mobilizing masses and hurl-
ing them against each other, was nationalism. The quarter century of
warfare that began in 1792 put an end to Europe as a way of life and
a mode of thinking shared by everyone in the educated elite. To make
contact with their common past, Europeans must therefore take a
great leap backward over the nineteenth and twentieth centuries and
reconsider the European dimension of life in the eighteenth century.

Not that anyone would want to revive the Old Regime. At that
time the vast majority of Europeans lived in misery. Most of them
east of the Elbe were serfs; most to the west lived in a state of intellectual serfdom, unable to read or to assert the rational maturity
(*Mündigkeit*) that Kant identified with Enlightenment. The Enlightenment itself was a complex movement, full of contradictions and
countercurrents. It never commanded the allegiance of a majority
among the elite, and it cannot be equated with all of intellectual life
in the eighteenth century. But it championed the values that lie at
the heart of the European Community today, and it did so in a way
that offers an alternative to nationalism—that is, it developed a pan-
European mode of existence known at the time as cosmopolitanism.

So much of the modern sense of self derives from identification with the nation that we can hardly imagine cosmopolitanism as a way of life. The eighteenth century provides instruction about that experience. Consider Prince Eugene of Savoy, for example. An Italian Frenchman who fought for Austria, he combined three languages in the signature of his name, Eugenio von Savoie. Frederick II of Prussia said that he spoke French to gentlemen and German to horses, while George I spoke German to his British subjects. Nationality had little meaning for such monarchs or for anyone else who commanded troops and directed diplomacy in the eighteenth century. War belonged to the game of balance of power, a matter of sieges and seasonal campaigns aimed at the capture of strategic positions rather than the conquest of nations.

It was a royal game, played in the name of dynasties: hence the wars of the Spanish Succession (1701–1714), the Polish Succession (1733–1738), and the Austrian Succession (1740–1748). Armies had no common uniform or flag. The foot soldiers included large proportions of foreigners, and the officers identified more with their opposite numbers among the enemy than with the men who fought under them. If captured, they were often swapped for prisoners of the same rank on the other side and returned at the end of the summer, when the fighting stopped and the opera season began.

Of course soldiers often suffered—thirty-four thousand men lay dead or wounded in ten square miles after the Battle of Malplaquet (1709), the bloodiest engagement before Borodino (1812; seventy-five thousand casualties)—but they did not fight for a cause or to annihilate an enemy, and civilians sometimes cheered for the other side. Voltaire congratulated Frederick II for defeating the French at Rossbach (1757), and Sterne remarked in his *Sentimental Journey* (1768), "I had left London [for Paris] with so much precipitation that it never entered my mind we were at war with France." The first stirrings of national sentiment can be detected in Britain and France during the Seven Years War (1756–1763), but Samuel Johnson expressed a common view when he defined "patriotism" as "the last refuge of scoundrels." (In fact, the "scoundrels" he had in mind were radicals who rallied around John Wilkes.)

An ideological interlude in the history of war took place between 1648, when the Peace of Westphalia marked the end of religion as a crucial element in international relations, and 1792, when the outbreak of the revolutionary wars signaled the beginning of wars between nations. During this period of relative civility the most civilized people thought of themselves as European and did not worry about national boundaries or even carry passports. They took grand tours, which led from London to Paris and Rome or through Amsterdam to Vienna or points north. Along the way they stopped in châteaux and town houses, where they received hospitality from other "persons of quality," who spoke the same language (French) and shared the same code of conduct, a matter of mastering not only the art of conversation but also body language: how to sit a horse, walk through a garden, enter a room, take a place at a table (no easy feat if you were wearing a sword), raise a glass of wine (by the stem with the thumb and two fingers, not three), and take tea (from the saucer, not the cup, in some refined circles).

Cosmopolitanism belonged to this social code. It set off persons of quality from the unwashed masses, whose mental horizon did not extend beyond the territory that could be viewed from the tower of their church; hence *l'esprit de clocher* (the bell tower spirit) and *campanilismo* (bell tower–ism) to denote the narrow-minded. The cosmopolitan took in all Europe, sometimes even all humanity, in his view of the world. The term could be used pejoratively, as indicated by the dictionary of the Académie française: "COSMOPOLITAN. Someone who does not adopt any fatherland. A cosmopolitan is not a good citizen." Even the *Encyclopédie* noted: "One sometimes uses this term in joking, to signify a man who has no fixed abode or a man who is not a foreigner anywhere." Adventurers like Casanova, Cagliostro, and Mesmer gave it a bad name, for they took grand tours of their own, living by their wits and the gullibility of their victims.

Having tramped around Europe with these *chevaliers d'industrie* in his youth, Rousseau in *The Social Contract* condemned the cosmopolitan as someone who "pretends to love the whole world in order to have the right to love no one." By contrast in this as in so many other things, Voltaire embodied the positive variety of cosmopolitanism. His estate at Ferney on the border between France and Geneva was the grandest stop on the grand tour. Flanked by busts of Locke and Newton, he received visitors from every corner of the Continent— and at least three hundred from Britain—so many secular pilgrims hungry for a meal or a *bon mot* that he described himself as "the innkeeper of Europe." He was described by others as "the uncrowned king of Europe" because he exerted a new kind of power, the ability to command public opinion on a European scale.

Voltaire's kingdom was actually a republic, the Republic of Letters. It extended everywhere and was open to everyone, or at least everyone connected with literature. With Pierre Bayle's *Nouvelles de la République des lettres* (1684–1687), it took on a tincture that distinguished it from its ancestor, the *Gelehrtenrepublik* of the sixteenth century. Under Bayle, it promoted the critical use of reason. Under Voltaire, it became engaged in the crusade against *l'infâme*—that is, against intolerance and injustice in general and the abuses of the Roman Catholic Church in particular. By the 1760s, therefore, the Republic of Letters was identified with the Enlightenment.

It had institutions: coffeehouses, Masonic lodges, salons, and academies, dozens of them, extending all the way to Saint Petersburg and bound together by correspondence networks. Writers located at nodal points in the system, like Samuel Formey, secretary of the Berlin Academy, spread messages on a vast scale and at remarkable speed. (Letters sometimes traveled faster in the eighteenth century than they do today.) Voltaire himself commanded

one of the most powerful networks of all time, and he used it to
pull strings everywhere in Europe. Artful doses of wit raised laughs
in all the salons of Paris and all the courts of Germany. Carefully
orchestrated denunciations of atrocities—the judicial murders of
Calas, La Barre, Lally-Tollendal, and Montbailli—turned laughter
into indignation. And direct appeals to the great—Frederick the
Great and Catherine the Great (187 letters exchanged with her
alone)—sometimes brought direct results.

This kind of Enlightenment worked from the top down, but it
could not succeed at a lower level unless it had some affinity with
the general culture of educated Europeans—culture in the broad-
est sense, as a way of being in the world. Like Norbert Elias,
Voltaire understood this culture as a civilizing process, which operated on a European scale: "Europeans are what the Greeks once
were. They make war among themselves, but in the midst of these
disputes, they conserve so much propriety and politeness that
when a Frenchman, an Englishman, and a German meet, they seem
to have been born in the same city."

Politeness lay at the heart of the Enlightenment's appeal to the
general public. Hume, Lessing, Beccaria, nearly all the *philosophes*
except Rousseau identified politeness with the conquest of superstition and barbarity. For them, Christianity was not merely unrea-
sonable; it was also vulgar. It derived from the crude world of the
ancient Hebrews. No gentleman could take it seriously. It was an
offense to taste.

The appeal to taste, a key word in the treatises as well as the correspondence of the *philosophes*, complemented the appeal to reason.
This dual strategy made the Enlightenment a force in eighteenth-
century Europe because at that time the gentleman was beginning
to displace the aristocrat as an ideal social type. There was room for
both in the genteel code of conduct, and both supplied demand
for the new trade in luxury goods. Ladies in London, Stockholm,

and Budapest learned the latest styles by studying dolls sent out every month from the couturiers of the rue Saint-Honoré. Palates were educated everywhere, thanks to treatises on the new art of *gastronomie* (a word invented in the eighteenth century) and new foods, like *pralines* (a neologism derived from the table of the duc de Praslin) and *mayonnaise* (invented by the chef of the duc de Richelieu at the siege of Fort Mahon). New kinds of furniture—the *commode*, the *secrétaire*—new hairstyles, porcelain, decorative arts of all kinds united the mixed elites of Europe in a common material culture.

The wealthy paid for their luxuries in different kinds of coins, but they usually kept their accounts in common units of currency that went back to Carolingian times. In Britain, France, and Italy, the pound, livre, or libra equaled twenty shillings, sols, or soldi, which in turn were worth twelve pence, deniers, or denari respectively—all abbreviated as £. s. d. Merchants used these units in bills of exchange, essentially promissory notes, which functioned like paper money and were used to settle accounts over vast distances. For example, F. Courtener, a bookseller in Moscow, wrote the following bill of exchange authorizing his Parisian merchant banker to pay for a shipment of books he had received from a Swiss publisher:

Moscow, 1 June 1792   *Good for £. 2539 tournois*
Twelve months from the date of the present, I will pay against this, my sole [bill] of exchange to the order of the Société typographique de Neuchâtel the sum of two thousand, five hundred, thirty-nine livres tournois in specie at the current rate for value received in merchandise.

F. Courtener

Bills of exchange circulated with the help of endorsements and discounting, and they ultimately had to be redeemed in local varieties of gold or silver coins. But they bound Europeans together in a system of credit that extended further than the euro does today.

The elites of Europe also shared a common language. French replaced Latin for the first time as the lingua franca of diplomacy in the Treaty of Rastadt (1714). By 1774 even the Russians and the Turks used French when they agreed on the text of a treaty. French tutors spread the language among the rich everywhere from Saint Petersburg to Naples, while the poor, even in France, remained divided by endless, mutually incomprehensible dialects When Gibbon was a student in Lausanne, it seemed natural for him to begin writing history in French "because I think in French." The same consideration prompted Pushkin to write his first poetry in French, which he called "the language of Europe." Frederick II, who perfected his French under the tutelage of Voltaire, ordered the Academy of Sciences in Berlin to publish its transactions in French, *"la langue universelle,"* in 1743. By 1782, when the academy sponsored its famous essay contest on the universality of the French language, Europe had been Frenchified.

Linguistic cosmopolitanism meant that publishing and bookselling operated on a European scale. Printers turned out books in French from shops in London, Amsterdam, Hamburg, Dresden, Geneva, and many other cities outside France. The best French newspapers—*La Gazette d'Amsterdam, La Gazette de Leyde, Le Courrier de l'Europe*—also were produced outside the kingdom. If reading them resulted in what Benedict Anderson calls an "imagined community," it was European before it was nationalistic. Voltaire's readers probably echoed his own sentiments: "I belong to Europe."

All the media contributed to this collective consciousness, even word of mouth. The art of conversation had been perfected in the Parisian salons of the seventeenth century. It served as a model for small talk in elegant circles everywhere, as Caraccioli explained in *Paris le modèle des nations étrangères, ou l'Europe française.* In it, a French marquis exclaims, "Italians, English, Germans, Spanish, Poles, Russians, Swedes, Portuguese . . . you are all my brothers."

Fraternity was a European-wide phenomenon before the Revolution incorporated it into the national culture of France. Of course it did not extend below the elite. Only gentlemen thought of themselves as united in a common way of life, and their participation in a European civilization did not preclude citizenship in a local community with its own culture expressed in an idiom of its own. Identity in the eighteenth century was segmental: A gentlemen belonged to a family, a corporate body, a town or region, and a country as well as to Europe. Which segment took priority in his mind varied from person to person. Squire Western can hardly be equated with Western civilization.

Yet the elites were opening up and expanding throughout the West. The new rich rubbed elbows with the gentlefolk in shops where a new consumer culture was taking root. Even artisans occasionally bought watches and wore swords. Even servant girls owned several dresses, often made of calico and dyed in bright colors, unlike the heavy black and brown woolens worn by domestics in the seventeenth century. The common people consumed the new luxury products imported from abroad: coffee, tea, chocolate, sugar, and tobacco. Those from the middle ranks of society spent some of their new wealth and their new leisure in coffeehouses, an institution open to anyone who could pay the fare.

After its creation in Constantinople in 1560, the coffeehouse proliferated in all European cities from the mid-seventeenth century. It first appeared in London in 1660. By 1663 London had 82 coffeehouses; by 1734, 551. Because of their free talk and virtuosi, they became known as "tattling universities." They also served as centers for political cabals, for they provided pamphlets and newspapers as well as drink. The first London daily began publication in 1702, long after the first daily newspaper in Germany (Leipzig, 1660) but long before the first in France (Paris, 1777). Print, talk, and coffee combined to create a powerful new force everywhere in Europe, public opinion, which took a radical turn in all the great cities.

It took many forms and came from many sources, but it con-
verged around one idea that resonated everywhere, happiness.
Europeans came to believe that they should enjoy life on earth
instead of enduring it in order to win a place in paradise after
death. Expanding economies brought the new consumer goods
within the range of many middle-class budgets. Even peasants
enjoyed better conditions: A warmer climate succeeded the
"little ice age" of the seventeenth century; new crops—turnips,
potatoes, beets—produced relief from chronic famines, and
life expectancy probably improved by about ten years between
1700 and 1800. Of course ideas did not grow out of the ground
like turnips, but improved conditions and a sunnier climate of
opinion made the Enlightenment thinkable among the general
public.

Among the elite, notions of happiness had spread from daring
thought experiments conducted by *esprits forts* and *libertins* in the
sixteenth and seventeenth centuries. The natural world appeared
in the works of Giordano Bruno, René Descartes, and Baruch
Spinoza as a rational order and a source of potential pleasure
rather than a vale of tears. Libertinism became identified with free
thought as well as free love. The greatest lover of the century
embodied both principles and strutted them on the stage in
Molière's *Don Juan*. To be sure, Molière punished his hero with
hellfire, but the punishment looked less convincing in Mozart's
version of the story, an *opera buffa*. And when Goldoni reworked it,
he made Don Juan die of natural causes, lightning rather than
divine anger.

In 1776 happiness ceased to be a privilege of the aristocracy. It
became a right of man, proclaimed to the world in the American
Declaration of Independence: "life, liberty, and the pursuit of happiness." Happiness rather than property. The substitution of one
term for another opened the way for the right of equal access to the

good things in life. The French Constitution of 1793 reaffirmed the rights of 1789, "equality, liberty, security, property," but it subordinated them to a principle announced in its first article: "The purpose of society is the common happiness." From social welfare to socialism the distance was not great, and it was covered between 1793 and 1848.

Of course 1848 looks impossibly remote in the age of the euro. Does the age of the Enlightenment have any relevance for the predicament of Europe in 2002? Not directly, but the eighteenth century can serve as a reminder that the nation was not always a fundamental unit of existence, and the principles of the Enlightenment are still alive today. What else can one invoke if one wants to protest against intolerance and torture, discrimination and censorship, abuses and injustice of all kinds? This argument, however, seems vulnerable to two objections.

First, the elitist character of the Enlightenment may undercut commitment to its values. If the Republic of Letters was not democratic, why celebrate its cosmopolitanism as an inspiration for a democratic Europe? Answer: The Frenchified, aristocratic Europe of the eighteenth century does not provide a model for the European Community today. It merely shows that Europeans once felt united by a common way of life. But could not this sense of participation in a shared civilization spread to all segments of society? Could not English serve as a lingua franca today just as well as French did two centuries ago? It need not obliterate other languages. There is plenty of room for other varieties of culture to flourish between the extremes of cosmopolitanism and *campanilismo*. Elitism provided a strategy for Voltaire in his fight against *l'infâme*, but there were other strategies available at that time, some of them democratic, some revolutionary, as the French proved in 1789.

Second, the Enlightenment may be accused of Eurocentrism, or worse: of perpetrating cultural hegemony in the guise of universalism. Answer: The Enlightenment certainly coincided with a second age of discovery, and enlightened explorers extended European empires. But philosophers like Condorcet and Raynal protested against the oppression of colonial peoples and especially against slavery. The colonized often turned European principles against their masters and found congruent principles within their own traditions. The rejection of human rights in the name of "Asiatic values" has served the purposes of Asian dictators, and the defenders of democracy in Asia have drawn on the Enlightenment heritage of Europe without compromising their commitment to values of their own.

President Kim Dae Jung of South Korea adopted this position when he accepted the Nobel Peace Prize in December 2000:

> In Asia, long before the West, the respect for human dignity was written into systems of thought, and intellectual traditions upholding the concept of "demos" took root. "The people are heaven, the will of the people is the will of heaven, revere the people as you would heaven." This was the central tenet in the political thoughts of China and Korea as early as 3,000 years ago. Five centuries later in India, Buddhism rose to preach the supreme importance of one's dignity and rights as a human being.
>
> There were also ruling ideologies and institutions that placed the people first. Mencius, disciple of Confucius, said: "The king is son of heaven. Heaven sent him to serve the people with just rule. If he fails and oppresses the people, the people have the right, on behalf of heaven, to dispose of him."
>
> And this, 2,000 years before John Locke expounded the theory of the social contract and civic sovereignty.

To understand principles as rooted in history is not to deny their validity. To point out their cultural dimension is not to relativize them out of existence. On the contrary, Europeans can take heart from the fact that Europe existed as a cultural entity long before it became a monetary zone. If they heed their history, they will find grounds for defending human rights—not that history teaches lessons, but rather that it shows how the civilizing process entailed a struggle against barbarism. That struggle still goes on, and Europeans still have cause to cry, *"Ecrasons l'infâme."*

4

THE PURSUIT OF
HAPPINESS: VOLTAIRE
AND JEFFERSON

THE IDEA OF HAPPINESS HAS BECOME SO DEEPLY EMBEDDED
IN AMERICAN CULTURE THAT IT SOMETIMES DISAPPEARS
FROM SIGHT. It is everywhere and nowhere, an implicit assumption that colors a world view, hardly an idea at all. But it took shape
as an idea centuries ago, and if seen from the perspective of the history of ideas, it has a long and impressive pedigree.

It appears among the ancients in the philosophies of Plato and
Aristotle and especially in the thought of the Epicureans and Stoics.
The Epicureans incorporated the concept of happiness into a general
philosophy of pleasure and pain, which led to an ethics of rational
self-interest. The Stoics linked it to withdrawal from the dangerous
hurly-burly of civic life and contentment in the minimal pleasures of
life in Arcadian retreats. "Happy is he who, far away from business,
like the race of men of old, tills his ancestral fields with his own
oxen, unbound by any interest to pay," said Horace in the first century B.C. One could find similar sentiments scattered throughout
the Augustan poetry and Ciceronian rhetoric of the Romans.

Not, however, among the early Christians. Before his death in
A.D. 604, Saint Augustine characterized life on this side of the City
of God as the pursuit of vanity through a vale of tears. His message
corresponded to the human condition as it was experienced by

most people for the next thousand years, when men and women
worked the fields in a state of semislavery, ate little more than bread
and broth, and died young. Theirs was an existence best summed up
by Thomas Hobbes's description of life in the state of nature: "soli-
tary, poor, nasty, brutish, and short."

By the fifteenth century, however, philosophers were facing a
revived notion of pleasure—earthly as in Boccaccio and refined as in
the court of the Medici. To be sure, the classical revival was snuffed
out in Florence by Savonarola's bonfire of vanities in 1497 and in
Rome by the troops of Charles V during the sack of 1527. The ref-
ormations and religious wars made happiness as a consummation to
be desired this side of the grave look more unlikely than ever.

But in the eighteenth century the idea of happiness revived once
again, attached to other notions such as progress and prosperity.
The Enlightenment philosophers took happiness to be the end of
man's life as an individual and of society's existence as a collectiv-
ity. The most radical of them, Diderot, Rousseau, Helvétius, and
d'Holbach, built the concept of happiness into a modernized Epi-
cureanism, reinforced with a strong civic consciousness.

Having reached this point, philosophy in the nineteenth and
twentieth centuries could not turn back, despite the countercurrents of pessimism stirred up by figures such as Nietzsche and
Freud. Jeremy Bentham's rallying cry, "the greatest happiness of the
greatest number," actually was formulated by two *philosophes* of the
Enlightenment, Francis Hutcheson in Scotland and Cesare Beccaria
in Italy. Bentham worked it into a philosophy of enlightened
self-interest derived from Epicurus and Lucretius and adapted to
the reform politics of Britain. For Karl Marx, the prophet of socialist happiness, liberal reforms could never reconcile individual and
collective interests because class interests stood in the way. Instead
Marx imagined happiness as a historical state to be reached at the
end of a dialectical process by society as a whole.

Such, in a snapshot, is how a history of the idea of happiness might look if seen at a very great distance, like the earth photographed from the moon. But from such a perspective, everything blurs into everything else. What would notions of happiness look like if seen up close? I should like to examine two such views located at what I consider the great turning point in the history of happiness, the second half of the eighteenth century. More precisely, I want to explore two famous phrases: "We must cultivate our garden," offered by Voltaire as the conclusion to *Candide* (1759), and the right to "the pursuit of Happiness," proclaimed by Jefferson in the American Declaration of Independence. The effort, I hope, will shed light on that curiously quicksilver phenomenon known as the American way of life.

The last line of *Candide,* "We must cultivate our garden," is the final remark in a philosophical discourse that accompanies a fast-moving, picaresque plot. Spoken by the chastened protagonist, it is meant to answer a question. But what was that question? None of the characters in the final chapter of the book asks Candide anything. They chatter past one another as they have done throughout the entire story. The question is provided by the story itself. In pursuing his true love, Cunégonde, from one adventure to another, Candide is pursuing happiness. How can happiness be found? That is the question posed by the novel, as by the entire French Enlightenment, and the answer can be reformulated as "Happiness lies in the cultivation of our garden."

Of the many glosses on the text, four stand out: stoic withdrawal (by shutting themselves up in the garden, Candide and his companions turn their backs on politics); pastoral utopianism (the little society supports itself by farming, cutting itself off from commercial capitalism); secular salvation through work (everyone in the group labors hard, thereby staving off poverty, boredom, and vice); and cultural *engagement* (cultivation means commitment to the cause of civilization). There is something to be said for each of these interpretations. Each fits the context of Voltaire's concerns in 1758 as he composed *Candide:* his quarrel with Frederick II; the horrors of the Seven Years War; the even more horrible disaster of the Lisbon earthquake; Voltaire's debate over the problem of evil with the followers of Leibniz and Wolff; and his recent decision to retire as a country gentleman to Les Délices, where he worked hard at creating a garden of his own.

The garden motif also summons up the Christian utopia of Eden, a favorite target of Voltaire in his youth. As a freethinking man-about-town in Regency Paris, he celebrated the pleasures of high society, or *le monde* and derided Christian asceticism. Thus, in his youthful credo, "Le Mondain," he mocked the barbarity of our mythical ancestors in a weedy, unkempt Garden. He pictured Adam as an ape-man dragging his knuckles on the ground and Eve as a foul-smelling slut with dirt under her fingernails. Instead of Eden, Voltaire celebrated the world of wit and beauty enjoyed by the rich and the wellborn in *le monde.* Happiness was to be found not in paradise but in Paris, not in the afterlife but in the here and now. "Terrestial paradise is where I am," concluded "Le Mondain." It was an Epicurean credo, flung in the face of the Church, and it captured the spirit of salon society in the early eighteenth century. But it had nothing to say to most of humanity, which lived in misery outside the salons.

By 1758 Voltaire had seen more of the world. But he did not cease to delight in the good things of life. The last chapter of *Candide* included a description of the hospitality offered by a philosophic Turk, whose little farm provided a model for Candide's: exquisite sorbet, a fine selection of fruits and nuts, "mocca coffee which was not mixed with the bad coffee of Batavia" (Voltaire was a coffee addict), courteous service by the two daughters of the host, and intelligent conversation. Candide had received the same kind of hospitality, though on a grander scale, from the philosopher-king of Eldorado, the utopian society described in the middle of the novel. Voltaire himself offered it to visitors at Les Délices and later at Ferney. What distinguished this kind of good life from the Epi-cureanism advocated by the young Voltaire in "Le Mondain"?

The setting, for one thing. Candide settled his community at the eastern edge of European civilization, just as Voltaire established his estate at the eastern boundary of France, far from Paris and far from politics. "I never inform myself about what is going on in Con-stantinople," the philosophic Turk tells Candide. Of course Voltaire worked hard to keep himself informed about intrigues in the French capital, but he had cut himself off from court life. He had withdrawn from *le monde,* and he had changed his tone. A new note of anger and darkness crept into all his writing after he fled from Frederick II and Berlin. He found himself increasingly confronted with unhappiness—and, worse, evil.

Consider one of the unhappiest moments in Voltaire's life. It occurred in 1730. His beloved mistress, the great actress Adrienne Lecouvreur, suddenly died after playing the lead in his tragedy *Oedipe.* Death struck Adrienne Lecouvreur before she had time to renounce her profession and receive Extreme Unction. As actors and actresses were excluded from the rites of the church, her body could not be buried in hallowed ground. Therefore it was dumped in a ditch and covered with quicklime to speed its decomposition.

This obscene act obsessed Voltaire right up to the moment of his own death, when he feared that his body would receive the same treatment. It appears in some of his most impassioned poetry, in the *Lettres philosophiques,* and even in *Candide.* In chapter 22, Can-dide visits Paris and is told the story in all its horror. He then remarks: "That [was] very impolite." Not what we would expect by way of a comment on a barbarism that had set a lover's blood to boil.

But Voltaire filled the word "politeness" with a passion that may escape the twentieth-century eye. The first characteristic Candide noticed among the inhabitants of the utopian society of Eldorado was their "extreme politeness." He marveled at their good manners, elegant clothing, sumptuous housing, exquisite food, sophisticated conversation, refined taste, and superb wit. The king of Eldorado epitomized those qualities. Like the philosophic Turk at the end of the book, he "received them with all imaginable grace and invited them politely to supper." Utopia is above all a *société polie* or *policée,* which amounts to the same thing.

The eighteenth-century notion of "police" could be translated roughly as rational administration. It belonged (conceptually, not etymologically) to a series of interlocking terms—*poli, policé, politique*—that extend from culture to politics. For Voltaire, the cultural system of the Old Regime shaded off into a power system, and the code of polite society belonged to the politics of enlightened absolutism.

The interpenetration of culture and politics is the main theme of Voltaire's most ambitious treatise, *Le Siècle de Louis XIV* (1751). This was a crucial work for eighteenth-century writers, a book that defined the literary system of the Old Regime and that created literary history in France. In it, Voltaire effectively argued that all history is literary history. Kings, queens, and generals do not count in the long run, although they attract most of the attention of their contemporaries and occupy a good deal of Voltaire's narrative. What matters above all is civilization. So, of the four "happy" ages in the history of mankind, the happiest of all was the age of Louis XIV, when French literature reached its zenith and the politeness (*"la politesse et l'esprit de société"*) of the French court set a standard for all Europe.

By "civilization," Voltaire meant the moving force in history, a combination of aesthetic and social elements, manners and mores (*moeurs*) that pushes society toward the ideal of Eldorado, a state in which men are perfectly *polis* and *policés*. So Voltaire understood *politesse* as power, and he saw an essential connection between classical French literature and the absolutism of the French state under Louis XIV. This argument underlies the key episodes of *Le Siècle de Louis XIV*. Louis masters the French language by studying the works of Corneille, he controls the court by staging plays, and he dominates the kingdom by turning the court itself into an exemplary theater. That idea may be a cliché now, but Voltaire invented it. He saw power as performance, the acting out of a cultural code. This code spread from Versailles to Paris, to the provinces, and to the rest of Europe. Voltaire does not deny the importance of armies, but he interprets the supremacy of Louis XIV as ultimately a matter of cultural hegemony. The script for his conquest at court was written by Molière, whom Voltaire describes both as a *philosophe* and as "the legislator of the code of conduct in polite society" (*le législateur des bienséances du monde*).

However anachronistic and inaccurate, this view of history conveys something more than the chase after the good things in life in "Le Mondain." It conveys direction, purpose, power—something akin to the "civilizing process" of Norbert Elias. It also demotes kings and puts *philosophes* in their place as the true masters of history, and it makes the historical process look progressive—uneven, to be sure, but one in which barbarism retreats before the forces of politeness.

Candide finally joins those forces. He becomes a *philosophe*—not a false philosopher, like his tutor Pangloss, but a true one, who opts for engagement instead of withdrawal. His pursuit of happiness, in the person of Cunégonde, does not lead to a happy ending. When he finally marries her, she has become ugly and disagreeable. But the pursuit has taught him to commit himself to something more substantial: polite society, or the process of civilization.

"THE PURSUIT OF HAPPINESS" is even more familiar to Americans than "We must cultivate our garden" is to the French. It is the most memorable phrase in the American Declaration of Independence, the rhetorical climax to Thomas Jefferson's enunciation of natural rights and revolutionary theory: "We hold these truths to be self-evident, that all men are created equal, that they are endowed by their Creator with certain inalienable Rights, that among these are Life, Liberty, and the pursuit of Happiness." What did Jefferson mean by "the pursuit of Happiness"? And what does his meaning have to do with a subject that belongs to the history of mentalities—namely, the American way of life?

Analysts of political discourse often determine meaning by showing what is not said as well as what is said. "Life, liberty, and property" was the standard formula in the political debates of the English-speaking world during the seventeenth and eighteenth centuries. In substituting "the pursuit of Happiness" for "property," the Declaration of Independence deviated significantly from other founding charters—the Petition of Right and the Declaration of Rights connected with the English revolutions of 1640 and 1688, for example, and the declarations of the American Stamp Act Congress of 1765 as well as the First Continental Congress of 1774. If "the pursuit of Happiness" is to be viewed as a speech act, its meaning must consist, at least in part, in an implicit comparison with the right of property. By omitting "property" from his phrasing, did Jefferson reveal himself to be a secret socialist? Can Americans cite him today in order to legitimate demands for social welfare legislation and to oppose the advocates of minimal, laissez-faire government?

Before we tear Jefferson out of the eighteenth century and plunge him into the midst of our own ideological quarrels, it would be wise to ask how "happiness" resonated in the context of his time. As a philosophically minded lawyer he had a thorough knowledge of the natural law tradition, which went back to Plato and Aristotle and was formulated for the law students of his generation by Locke, Pufendorf, Burlamaqui, and Blackstone. The most important of these was Locke. (Jefferson had a personal distaste for Blackstone's *Commentaries.*) In fact, Locke was so important that many scholars have considered him the grandfather of the American Declaration of Independence, which advanced a contractual theory of government that seemed to come straight out of his *Second Treatise on Civil Government* (1690).

The *Second Treatise* certainly provides grounds for asserting a right to revolution if the government violates its contractual obligations to the citizenry. But a right to happiness? Locke kept to the usual trinity: "life, liberty, and property." In his *Essay concerning Human Understanding* (1690), however, he stretched "property" into "lives, liberties, and estates," and then went on to talk of "that property which men have in their persons as well as goods." In doing so, he shifted ground from law to psychology. Property in one's person implied the liberty to develop the self, and self-development for Locke was an epistemological process. It took place when men combined and reflected on sensations, the primary signals of pleasure and pain, according to the procedure described in the *Essay.* Thus the sensationalism of Locke's epistemology could be combined with the natural rights of his political theory in a way that would open the road to the right to happiness. In short, Locke too was a philosopher of happiness. He said so himself: "As therefore the highest perfection of intellectual nature lies in a careful and constant pursuit of true and solid happiness, so the care of ourselves that we mistake not imaginary for real happiness is the necessary foundation of our liberty."

But Jefferson did not need to combine passages from the two John Lockes, the Locke of the *Second Treatise* and the Locke of the *Essay concerning Human Understanding,* because the work had already been done for him by his friend George Mason. Mason was the one who did the most to stretch "property" into "happiness" in the philosophical deliberations of Virginia's radical squierearchy. Like Jefferson, Mason had a library packed with the works of philosophers, ancient and modern, in Gunston Hall, his country estate. Having worked through this material while participating in the agitation over the Stamp Act, Mason drafted a series of manifestos about representative government and natural rights. He discussed them with like-minded country gentlemen—George Washington, Thomas Jefferson, James Madison, Patrick Henry—around dinner tables and through correspondence. He debated them in freeholder meetings, held in the brick courthouse of Fairfax Country, in 1774 and 1775.

Then, in May 1776, the Virginians met at Williamsburg and declared themselves independent of Great Britain. Mason provided the philosophic justification for this revolutionary step by drafting a Declaration of Rights, which included the phrase "All men are created equally free and independent, and have certain inherent natural rights . . . among which are the enjoyment of life and liberty, with the means of acquiring and possessing property, and pursuing and obtaining happiness and safety." Mason's wording runs exactly parallel to the famous phrase that Jefferson wrote into the Declaration of Independence a few weeks later. It suggests that happiness is not opposed to property but is an extension of it.

Jefferson made no pretense to originality. He described his statement of principles as the mere "common sense of the subject." A half century later, when he discussed the Declaration of Independence in a letter to James Madison, he explained further: "Neither aiming at originality of principle or sentiment, nor yet copied from any particular and previous writing, it was intended to be an expression of the American mind."

"Common sense" and "the American mind": We are entering territory that the French call the history of mentalities, and that I should prefer to describe as anthropological history. The American anthropologist Clifford Geertz has analyzed common sense as a "cultural system"—that is, as an admixture of attitudes, values, and cognitive schemata that ordinary people use to make sense of the world. Ordinary people, not philosophers. True, Jefferson, Madison, Mason, and their crowd look like American-style *philosophes.* And when compared with today's statesmen, they look like giants. But they were also Virginia farmers who inhabited a commonsense world of tobacco plantations, Georgian manor houses, Episcopal churches, county courts, taverns, horse races, and (let us not forget it) slavery. The plantations kept them separated from one another in semiautonomous units ordered according to patriarchal principles. The churches and courthouses drew them together in settings that reinforced the social hierarchy. The taverns and horse races gave them a chance to vent their passions and strut their status. And the slavery indicated the limitations of statements such as "all men are created equal."

This contradiction did not weigh too heavily with men who thought of themselves as successors to the slaveholding patricians of Augustan Rome. Their libraries confirmed the message of their larders. The classicism of their education echoed the classical architecture of their houses. Cicero and Seneca rang true because they conformed with the values of order and hierarchy given off by the everyday surroundings in Virginia. So did Locke, the spokesman of a Whig aristocracy aligned against an alien, absolutist monarchy. In short, the philosophizing fitted the social environment, not as an ideological afterthought but as the reflective gentleman's way of making sense of what his common sense already proclaimed. "Sense" in this respect belonged to what Max Weber called *Sinnzusammenhang,* or "elective affinities"; it was a way of ordering reality.

How did the Virginians describe reality in more casual moments, when they were not composing theoretical manifestos? Here is Jefferson again, writing from his country estate in 1810:

> I am retired to Monticello, where, in the bosom of my family, and sur-rounded by my books, I enjoy a repose to which I have been long a stranger. My mornings are devoted to correspondence. From breakfast to dinner, I am in my shops, my garden, or on horseback among my farms; from dinner to dark, I give to society and recreation with my neighbors and friends; and from candle light to early bedtime, I read. My health is perfect; and my strength considerably reinforced by the activity of the course I pursue. . . . I talk of ploughs and harrows, of seeding and harvesting, with my neighbors, and of politics too, if they choose, with as little reserve as the rest of my fellow citizens, and feel, at length, the blessing of being free to say and do what I please.

This is happiness, something embedded in the daily course of life. It is an American way of life—but closer to Horace and Virgil than to the America of Madison Avenue and Wall Street.

Also, it should be added, the Horatian glow dimmed during the next sixteen years, a period when Monticello nearly collapsed into bankruptcy and its master felt increasingly alienated from the Jacksonian variety of politics, a speculative surge of capitalism, and an evangelical revival of religion. By cultivating his garden in Monticello, Jefferson withdrew from the world—unlike Voltaire, who used Ferney as a fortress for conquering it.

If Jefferson himself found an increasing disparity between his ideals of the 1770s and the realities of the 1820s, how did Americans see any continuity at all between his way of life and theirs during the next century and a half? Horatian Jeffersonianism and industrial capitalism seem so far apart that one would think they have nothing in common. Yet they are bound together by a common thread, the pursuit of happiness.

As the intellectual historian Howard Mumford Jones has shown, that theme provides one of the leitmotifs of American jurisprudence. If, as the Declaration of Independence proclaims, I have a right to happiness, shouldn't the courts enforce it? Unfortunately, the Declaration of Independence did not become part of constitutional law, except as it was rewritten in the form of the Bill of Rights, and the Bill of Rights does not mention happiness. The state constitutions, however, do. Two-thirds of them have adopted some variant of Jefferson's phrase. So for more than a century Americans have gone to court, suing their authorities and one another over a right they believe belongs to them by fundamental law. They have claimed the right to happiness in order to set up massage parlors, sell contraceptives, and smoke opium. They have rarely succeeded, but their attempts indicate the prevalence of a general attitude that the pursuit of happiness is a basic ingredient of the American way of life.

Of course a great deal besides constitutional law went into this cultural pattern. The open frontier, the availability of land, the gold rush, the seemingly endless opportunities for getting rich and getting ahead:——all oriented values around the notion of happiness in the nineteenth century. In each case happiness appeared as something to be pursued, not something showered down from heaven, and the pursuit often led westward. In this respect the Jeffersonian ideal also provided a jumping-off point because the agrarian, yeoman democracy favored by Jefferson provided the ideological impulse for the conquest of the frontier. In the Northwest Territory Act and the Louisiana Purchase, Jefferson himself tried to shape the settlement of the West in a way that would perpetuate the society of farmer-*philosophes* he had known in Virginia. Horace Greeley and other publicists echoed this idea when they proclaimed, "Go West, young man!"

The real impulse, however, was money, money and land, the chance to get rich quick. The gold rush precipitated a general *Drang nach Westen.* Ever since 1848 it has seemed that the whole country has tried to move to California. I am exaggerating, of course, because the great waves of immigrants who were carried across the Atlantic during the late nineteenth and early twentieth centuries generally washed onto the East Coast and emptied themselves in the slums between Boston and Baltimore. Many of the poor from Kiev and Naples never got farther west than the East Side of Manhattan, although their descendants usually crossed the Hudson and settled in the suburbs of New Jersey—not exactly in Jeffersonian freeholds but on their own plots of land, in houses with gardens and white picket fences, which turned into the new version of the American dream. To such people, America really was the land of opportunity, even if it took two generations to extricate themselves from the slums, even if suburbia was a far cry from the Oregon Trail.

Thus did the Jeffersonian vision become transformed into the American dream, a vision that was basically materialistic but that inflamed imaginations throughout the Old World, where millions struggled to get out and to get ahead. The dream is still alive today, although the immigrants generally come from Latin America and settle in Miami, Houston, and Los Angeles. But its realization remains an elusive goal to many African Americans, whose ancestors—who did the work on Jefferson's plantation—were legally excluded from its pursuit and who provided a living witness to the tragic flaw in the American dream.

That did not prevent the dream from gathering more force in the second half of the twentieth century. Technology seemed to bring happiness within the reach of nearly everyone, because it provided the means of controlling the environment, of enjoying pleasure and mitigating pain. The point may be so obvious that we cannot see it, as we have become insulated from the pains of everyday life that existed in the age of Jefferson. Having read thousands of letters from the eighteenth century, I often think of the dread of

rotting teeth, the horror of the itinerant tooth puller, the sheer pain
in jaws everywhere in the early modern world. Dentistry may not
look like a particularly noble calling, but it has weighed heavier
than many professions in the hedonistic calculus we have inherited
from Epicurus and Jeremy Bentham.

To dentistry, add medicine in general, vaccination, public
hygiene, contraception, insurance, retirement benefits, unemploy-
ment compensation, lightning rods, central heating, air condition-
ing. . . . The list could go on forever because it leads through the
endless array of goods we associate with the so-called consumer
society and the services we expect of the "welfare state." I know
that these are hard times for millions of Americans and that my
remarks may sound hollow. But I have spent so much time in the
eighteenth century that I cannot fail to be impressed with how
much control man has gained over his environment in the nineteenth and twentieth centuries.

The pursuit of happiness in America has spilled over from science
and technology into popular culture, a favorite subject for historians of mentality. The most exotic varieties bloom in Southern
California: hot tubs, "perfect" waves, "deep" massage, fat farms,
love clinics, and therapy of every conceivable kind, not to mention
the happy endings that still prevail in Hollywood. This kind of popular culture can easily be caricatured, but it cannot be dismissed
easily because it has spread throughout the country and now the
world. One encounters the face of "Joe Happy"—a circle with a
smile in it—everywhere: pasted on windows, pinned in button-
holes, even, I have found, dotting the *i*'s in students' papers. Along
with the current greeting—"have a nice day"—it expresses the
thumbs-up, bright-eyed and bushy-tailed form of public behavior
that can be so annoying to Europeans, who prefer the limp hand-
shake, the down-at-the-mouth Gauloise, and the café slouch as a
style of self-presentation.

Of course, many other strains run through the patterns of culture in everyday America, and many run counter to the pursuit of happiness. In order to situate the motif of happiness within the pattern as a whole, it is important to keep three considerations in mind. First, America has always contained a vocal minority of cockeyed pessimists. The American jeremiad arrived on the *Mayflower,* along with sermonizing about the "City on a Hill," or colony of saints. While Thomas Jefferson expanded on Locke, Jonathan Edwards defined happiness as follows:

> The sight of hell torments will exalt the happiness of the saints forever. It will not only make them more sensible of the greatness and freeness of the grace of God in their happiness; but it will really make their happiness the greater, as it will make them more sensible of their own happiness; it will give them a more lively relish of it.

Americans have been avid consumers of antiutopian literature: *1984, Animal Farm, Brave New World,* and dark varieties of science fiction. They also have produced a vast amount of pessimistic literature, from Hawthorne and Melville to T. S. Eliot, Kurt Vonnegut, and John Updike. The Civil War, the closing of the frontier, the Great Depression, the Beat Generation, and the antiwar activists of the 1960s represented so many stages of disillusionment with the American dream. Most young people today believe they live in a world of limited resources rather than unlimited opportunity. Public opinion polls indicate that they do not expect to do better than their parents. If they no longer worry about a nuclear catastrophe and the Cold War, they sense economic contraction and ecological disaster everywhere. In the face of the AIDS epidemic, many of them feel angry—at the government and at the world in general, for AIDS represents the ultimate denial of the pursuit of happiness as a way of life.

Second, those who continue to believe in happiness as an end often pursue it with an earnestness that looks self-contradictory. They take up extreme forms of asceticism. They diet; they jog; they lift weights; they deprive themselves of tobacco, meat, butter, and all the pleasures that Falstaff categorized under the rubric "cakes and ale." To what end? To live forever? Aging has now become a major industry in America, and the American way of life has evolved into the American way of death—that is, the subculture of funeral "homes" and pastoral cemeteries that dress death up so prettily as to deny it. But most of America's worldly ascetics have transformed the old Protestant ethic into a new cult of the self. *Self* magazine, the "me generation," and the appeals to building a better body and developing a more assertive or better-balanced personality all express a general egoism that looks like the opposite of the Stoical and Puritanical varieties of self-discipline practiced by the Founding Fathers.

Egocentric asceticism brings us to the third point, John Kenneth Galbraith's characterization of the American way of life as "private wealth and public squalor." Despite food stamps and Social Security, the welfare state never made much headway in the United States. True, the national parks and some of the state systems of higher education opened the door to happiness for many millions. But the consumer culture (we do not have a national sales tax) and the cult of rugged individualism (we do not wait in line at bus stops) stood in the way of state-sponsored projects to assure a minimal degree of happiness for the entire population.

Roosevelt's New Deal, launched to the tune of "Happy Days Are Here Again," provided no answer to the problems of poverty and racism. Those problems continue to fester at the center of our cities, while individuals pursue their personal welfare in the private enclosures of our suburbs. It is, I believe, a national disgrace, but it is also a general problem, one that goes back to the opposition between the private and the public varieties of happiness that were incarnated in Voltaire and Rousseau, and back even farther to the Epicureans and the traditions of antiquity. While remaining rooted in the Jeffersonian tradition, the American pursuit of happiness shares promises and problems that have characterized Western civilization in general.

What to make of it all? The leitmotifs in patterns of culture do not lead to bottom lines, so I shall not try to end with a firm conclusion. Instead let me cite two examples of the pursuit of happiness I recently came upon. The first expresses the technical, commercial, and individualistic strain. Dr. Raymond West announced a couple of years ago that "happiness is a warm stethoscope," and offered a new invention to an astonished world: a stethoscope warmer, which would make health checkups more pleasurable and abolish forever the unpleasurable sensation of "ice cubes on the back."

The second example is less trivial. It expresses the collective end of the American republic as it was originally defined by Thomas Jefferson, and it comes from the inaugural address President Clinton delivered in January 1993: "When our founders boldly declared America's independence to the world and our purposes to the Almighty, they knew that America, to endure, would have to change. Not change for change's sake, but change to preserve America's ideals—life, liberty, the pursuit of happiness."

Noble words. But Clinton would have done well to think of Washington as well as Jefferson: Washington the statesman and Washington the victim of tooth decay. Imagine Washington sitting down to a banquet in Candide's garden. If we are ever to bring together the two ways of pursuing happiness, the individual and the social, we should follow Washington's example, set our jaws firmly, grit our teeth, tuck in, and dedicate ourselves to the public welfare. Such, at least, is the view of one American at a moment when the welfare state looks as beleaguered as Monticello.

5

THE GREAT DIVIDE:
ROUSSEAU ON THE
ROUTE TO VINCENNES

EVERY AGE CREATES ITS OWN ROUSSEAU. We have had Rousseau
the Robespierrist, the romantic, the progressive, the totalitarian,
and the neurotic. I should like to propose Rousseau the anthropologist. He invented anthropology as Freud invented psychoanalysis,
by doing it to himself. Nothing that he wrote would meet the professional standards of the *American Anthropologist*. But if we reread
his writings with a fresh eye, we might learn what it is to live the
contradictions of a cultural system and to overcome them by
understanding culture itself.

Of course anthropology has other founding fathers. But its
genealogy looks different now that the academic disciplines are
grouping into new configurations. In place of the old tripartite divi-
sion—natural sciences, social sciences, humanities—a new coali-
tion of the human sciences is beginning to emerge. It brings
together disciplines concerned with the interpretation of culture—
certain varieties of anthropology, sociology, history, literary criticism, and philosophy—as against those devoted to the uncovering
of behavioral laws. Instead of searching for the causes of events, the
new humanists attempt to understand the workings of symbolic
systems. They try to think themselves into alien ways of thought
and to see how ways of thinking shape patterns of behavior. They

study culture as an activity rather than as an inert body of ideas—
as something closer to the stuff of politics than to the stock of
museums. And so they should be ready to reconsider Rousseau.

Rousseau first collided with the central problems of the human
sciences on a hot afternoon in the summer of 1749. He was hiking
from Paris to Vincennes, where he planned to visit his friend Denis
Diderot. The five-mile route led past the Hôpital des Enfants Trouvés, where Rousseau had abandoned his illegitimate children, to
the medieval fortress where Diderot was then imprisoned for publishing his impious *Letters on the Blind.* As the sun beat down on him,
Rousseau skimmed a copy of a literary journal that he had brought
to read along the way. His eye stopped at the announcement of a
question proposed by the Academy of Dijon for an essay contest:
"Has the revival of the arts and sciences contributed to the purifi-
cation of morals?"

> As soon as I read it, I saw another universe and I became another man.
> . . . Unable while walking to breathe anymore, I let myself fall beneath
> one of the trees along the avenue; and I spent a half hour there in such
> a state of agitation that when I got up I noticed the front of my coat
> was completely soaked with my tears although I hadn't known I was
> weeping. . . . If I could have written but a fraction of what I saw and
> felt under that tree, how clearly would I have exposed the contradic-
> tions of the social system.

History has been stingy with eureka moments. We think of
Archimedes in his bath, Paul en route to Damascus, Newton under-
neath the apple tree; but even if such scenes actually occurred, they
come down to us surrounded by so much mythology that we tend
to discount them. Rousseau certainly made a myth of his life. Yet we
cannot slice through the *Confessions* separating rhetoric from reality,
because Rousseau fashioned his self with his fiction. Better to take

him at his word and with his words and to ask why the question posed on the road to Vincennes seemed so significant to him. For Rousseau translated it into personal terms: What is the sense of my life? What has gone wrong with it? The search for an answer would lead from his obscure origins to "the contradictions of the social system"—ultimately, that is, to anthropology.

Rousseau's itinerary through eighteenth-century society is astounding, even if one makes allowances for the mythical element in his account of it. The son of a watchmaker in the tiny republic of Geneva, he began life at a modest position in the social hierarchy and soon sank to the bottom. His mother died, his father disappeared, his relatives arranged apprenticeships with a lawyer and an engraver, but the boy would not be disciplined. One Sunday evening, when he was playing with some friends outside the city walls, he heard the call for curfew. They raced for the gate. Too late: It had slammed shut. They would have to spend the night outdoors and take a beating for their negligence the next morning. Having been caned twice for that offense, fifteen-year-old Jean-Jacques turned his back on Geneva and took to the open road.

He lived off and on it for the next thirteen years. As a paid convert to Catholicism, in Turin, he learned the price of his soul: twenty livres (about three weeks' wages for an unskilled laborer). As a lackey in a noble household he measured the distance between the extremes of gentility and villainy and saw where he belonged. Tramping back over the Alps, he concocted a plan to bamboozle meals from peasants by exhibiting a *fontaine de Héron,* which seemed to turn water into wine. Back in Annecy, he moved in with Mme. de Warens without becoming either a hired man, as he did nothing to earn his bread, or a kept man, as he called her Maman between the sheets.

On a jaunt through Switzerland he took a room at an inn, filled his belly, and announced the next morning that he could not pay his bill. Farther down the road he supported himself by giving music lessons, though he could barely read a score. He actually staged a concert in Lausanne, using a false name, but the musicians laughed him off the podium. Eventually he found a better source of cash, a self-proclaimed archimandrite of the Greek Orthodox Church who was collecting funds to restore the holy sepulcher in Jerusalem.

Serving as an interpreter and advance man, Rousseau led the Greek on a merry tour through Fribourg, Bern, and Solothurn. At the last stop the French ambassador, who had served in Constantinople, saw through the archimandrite's disguise and sent him packing. But Rousseau managed to turn this setback to his profit. By a well-timed confession he won the protection of the ambassador and left Solothurn with a hundred francs and letters of recommendation for a job as a tutor in Paris.

Up to this point the story might seem to fit the pattern of many picaresque narratives. If Mark Twain had told it, it would have come out sounding like the adventures of the Duke and the King in *Huckleberry Finn*. If it had come from the pen of Voltaire, it would have turned into a series of insults—apostate, lackey, thief, gigolo, confidence man—strung out in rhyming couplets, as in *The Poor Devil*. But in Rousseau's version the story has a strange, poetic quality. It is an idyll of lost innocence. And it has a social dimension that has escaped the attention of most commentators.

The first half of the *Confessions* takes us through all the strata of a highly stratified society, from the world of handworkers and servants to that of aristocrats and ambassadors. It also carries us outside the hierarchy of well-defined social "estates" and into the floating population of the Old Regime. Itinerant craftsmen, migrant laborers, beggars, deserters, actors, mountebanks, thieves: these drifters flooded the social landscape. They included a peculiar subspecies, the intellectual tramp, who lived by his wits, amusing, seducing, peddling, tutoring, and capturing confidence wherever there was a protector to be wooed or a penny to be made.

Intellectual tramps swarm through the early chapters of the *Confessions,* especially in Rousseau's account of the household of Mme. de Warens, which he remembered as a Garden of Eden that was continually being invaded by serpents: Bagueret, a confidence man who battened onto her purse after having failed to make his fortune at the court of Peter the Great; Wintzenried, an itinerant coiffeur who had learned to talk like a Parisian *bel-esprit* by seducing a string of marquises; and, above all, Venture de Villeneuve, a wandering musician whose knock at the door one wintry evening in 1730 echoed in Rousseau's memory as the fatal summons to Paris.

According to Rousseau's reconstruction of him, Venture was pure Parisian—badly tattered but well tailored and full of talk about actresses, operas, and boulevards. He set Jean-Jacques's head spinning. To cut a figure in the capital of the Republic of Letters! What glory could be greater? Young Rousseau tried to refashion himself on the Parisian model. With help from Maman, he bought the correct costume, learned to wear a sword, took dancing lessons, and studied music. For a while Rousseau roomed with Venture, and even adopted part of Venture's name as an alias—Vaussore de Villeneuve—when he left on his flimflamming tour as a music teacher in Switzerland. That road led inevitably to Paris—not the gilded Paris of the salons, however, but the Paris of Grub Street.

Armed with his letters of recommendation, Rousseau made a few attempts to break into the salons. But when he reported to Mme. Bezenval, her first thought was to send him to eat in the servants' quarters. Mme. de Boze admitted him to her table. But when she passed him some food, he speared a morsel with his fork instead of first taking the plate and then serving himself—a gaffe that she registered by a snicker at her servants behind his back. Of such small wounds is class consciousness created. Despite his tutelage with Maman, Rousseau felt them every day. He retained too much dirt under his fingernails to master the code of high society (*le monde*). So he retreated to neutral territory like the Café

Maugis, where he became a regular at the chessboards, and the cabaret of Mme. La Selle, where he listened to young men of quality boast about their adventures with dancers from the opera. The adventures often ended with the dumping of a baby at the Enfants Trouvés. So Rousseau had an example to follow when his own mistress became pregnant.

Thérèse Le Vasseur did not dance in the opera. She did the laundry in Rousseau's boardinghouse, and she failed to understand when he explained how the *honnêtes gens* disposed of their offspring. Her mother finally brought her around. The old woman recognized that Rousseau was a *Monsieur* who, if firmly attached, might pull the whole family out of indigence. Not that Jean-Jacques had accumulated any money. He had failed to flog his system of musical annotation, failed to find a patron for an opera, and failed to get his play *Narcissus* performed at the Comédie italienne. But after abandoning hope of making a splash in *le monde* as a literary figure, he landed a secretarial job in the wealthy household of Mme. Dupin. It brought in nine hundred livres a year, enough to keep Thérèse and to feed most of her family.

Such was Rousseau's situation in October 1749, when he set out to visit Diderot in Vincennes. Diderot's circumstances hardly looked better. Like Rousseau, he came from a family of artisans. He had failed to rise very high in the Republic of Letters and had cast his lot with a woman from a very low point in the social order—the daughter of a laundress—whom he not only loved but actually married. The two men struggled against the same odds in the same milieu. As he sweated along the road to Vincennes, Rousseau saw his friend as a victim of despotism. Years later, when he looked back on their life together in Grub Street, Diderot saw Rousseau as a nephew of Rameau.

That last point may be impossible to prove, at least to the satisfaction of the army of Diderot experts. But I see some striking

similarities between the antihero of *Rameau's Nephew* and the hero
of Rousseau's *Confessions*. Both were musicians. Both were addicted
to chess. Both were half-mad geniuses and spectacular eccentrics.
Both lived on the fringes of polite society, subsisting on scraps cast
off by the rich and powerful. And both undermined conventional
morality, first by confessing their own degradation, then by exposing the hypocrisy of the code by which they stood condemned.
Whether Rousseau actually served as a model for Diderot's mas-
terpiece remains an "academic" question. But by imagining
Rousseau as Rameau's nephew, one can form some idea of his state
of mind as he walked toward Vincennes. He was wandering in
a moral wilderness, and he arrived, as he put it, "in a ferment
bordering on delirium."

HAD THE PROGRESS of the arts and sciences corrupted or purified
morals? The question posed by the Academy of Dijon cut to the
heart of Rousseau's existence. But he did not put his answer in personal terms; not yet. Nor did he adopt the simple position sometimes attributed to him: Man is naturally good, society bad. The
Discourse on the Arts and Sciences advanced a subtler argument, which
would run through all of Rousseau's subsequent writing: Culture
corrupts, and absolutist culture corrupts absolutely.

Instead of romanticizing about a primitive state of nature,
Rousseau saw that morality was a cultural code, the unwritten
rules of conduct, knowledge, and taste that held society together.
Man could not do without it, for man stripped of culture was a
Hobbes-ian brute, lacking an ethical existence. But supercivilized
man, the *homme du monde* who divided his time between the opera
and the Cabaret La Selle, was still worse. Rousseau knew. He had
tried to become that man. By civilizing himself, he had come to
recognize civilization for what it was, a process of corruption. That

recognition hit him all at once on the route to Vincennes. When he staggered off the road, he stepped outside the dominant culture of his time and made himself into the first anthropologist.

Of course Rousseau did not express his insight in the language of Lévi-Strauss. Although he drew on the anthropological strain in French literature, especially on the ideas of Montaigne and Montesquieu, he wrote a jeremiad, a work of pure rhetoric and of such poetic power that it overwhelmed his readers. To the conventional images of his time—Oriental sages and Roman sophisticates—he opposed pictures of simple, vigorous folk—Frankish warriors, American Indians, republican Swiss and Dutch. Sparta vanquished Athens, and Rousseau rejoiced: "Oh Sparta, eternal opprobrium of a vain doctrine!" "Oh virtue, sublime science of simple souls . . ." The declamations may sound hollow today, but two and a half centuries ago they rang out as a bold challenge to the prevailing cultural tone—the *bon ton* of the salons. Rousseau attacked it openly. He excoriated "taste," "politeness," "urbanity," and the *beaux-esprits* who "smile disdainfully at those old words fatherland and religion." The arts and sciences were at bottom political institutions. The sophistication of the salons reinforced the despotism of Versailles. And all the men of letters who performed in the salons stood condemned as agents of corruption, all "except for one"—namely, Diderot.

Rousseau's outburst can be read as an indictment of the *Encyclopédie* of Diderot and d'Alembert, which bore the subtitle "Reasoned Dictionary of the Arts and Sciences." But the Encyclopedists held together and even prospered for a few years after the publication of the *Discourse on the Arts and Sciences*. Diderot, released from prison, saw the first volumes of the *Encyclopédie* into print and through increasing storms of controversy. Rousseau continued to contribute articles. And in the "Preliminary Discourse" to the *Encyclopédie,* d'Alembert dismissed Rousseau's essay as an eloquent paradox, which Rousseau had renounced by collaborating with the Encyclopedists.

Literary notoriety now made Rousseau into a collaborator of salon society as well. Great ladies snapped him up. Patrons opened their purses. The king's mistress herself intervened to have his opera *Le Devin du village* performed before the court. Soon Rousseau found himself about to be presented to the king and supported by a royal pension. The success of his attack on *le monde* had made him a captive of it, and so he faced a second crisis, one that led to his final break with the cultural system of the Old Regime.

Rousseau's success only confirmed his diagnosis of his failure. When he returned from his forays into the salons, he brooded on what was happening to him and to Thérèse. She became pregnant for the third time while he was working on his second discourse, the *Discourse on the Origins of Inequality,* which he submitted for a prize offered by the Academy of Dijon in 1754. The second essay went much further and deeper than the first. It opened with an impassioned dedication to the republic of Geneva, which Rousseau imagined as a Calvinist Sparta, and went on to expose social inequality as a product of the same civilizing process that he had denounced in his first discourse. Yet Rousseau composed it while lying on his bed and dictating to Thérèse's mother, who served him as secretary, maid, and accomplice in arranging the abandonment of his children.

In his *Preface to Narcissus* (1753), Rousseau had proclaimed that he would abandon his frivolous early works as if they were so many illegitimate children. Now he was producing more proclamations and abandoning more children. His moralizing had become fashionable. He was a fashion himself, a kind of wild animal captured from the lower ranks of society and exhibited for the fascination of those at the top. By parading his boorishness and playing the role of a "bear," as he was known, Rousseau collaborated in this game:

"Thrown into *le monde* without having the right tone and without being able to acquire it . . . I pretended to despise the politeness that I could not practice." Celebrity had transformed the intellectual tramp and Grub Street hack into a dancing bear.

In the process, Rousseau lost something: his self, the original Jean-Jacques of his fabled Geneva. When the sense of loss became unbearable, he broke with *le monde*. First he changed his dress. He renounced his wig, his sword, his white stockings, his watch, and (with the help of a thief) his forty-two fine linen shirts. He refused to lobby for the royal pension. He quit his job and took up copying music for a pittance a page. Finally, in April 1756, he left Paris. Installed with Thérèse in a cottage provided by Mme. d'Epinay in the park of Montmorency, he began the feverish period of writing that was to end six years later after the publication of three books that changed the course of cultural history: *La Nouvelle Héloïse,* *Émile,* and *The Social Contract.*

Each of those books developed an aspect of Rousseau's revelation on the route to Vincennes. Each cut to the heart of conventional wisdom on a major topic: literature, education, and politics. But the deepest cut of all came in a fourth book, the most unconventional and the most painful, for it consummated Rousseau's break with *le monde* by severing his ties with his *philosophe* friends, notably Diderot. This work, *Letter to M. d'Alembert on the Theater* (1759), was a passionate protest, which ran on for more than a hundred pages, against the suggestion that a theater be established in Geneva. D'Alembert had slipped the suggestion into his article on Geneva in the *Encyclopédie,* and Rousseau flayed away at it as if it were the wickedest idea in the wickedest century of history.

Why? Why did this composer of plays and operas fly into a fury at the seemingly innocent proposal to erect a stage in his hometown? Behind d'Alembert, Rousseau saw Voltaire, who was then living just outside Geneva; behind Voltaire, he saw Diderot and all the other Encyclopedists; behind them, the world of sophisticated Parisian culture; and behind that, the political system of the Old Regime. Everything interpenetrated everything else, and the force that held it all together was culture.

Rousseau therefore looked upon the theater as a profoundly political institution, and he condemned the high priests of the stage—Voltaire, d'Alembert, and Diderot as agents of political corruption. He conceded that the theater could have a place in the monarchy of France. By refining taste and corrupting morals it reinforced the Louis Quatorzean blend of aristocracy and authoritarianism. If injected into Geneva, however, it would poison the body politic. For republics did not draw their life from free elections, but from republican political culture—a matter of fraternizing in clubs, competing in outdoor games, and joining the chorus in the civic festivals that Rousseau was to idealize in *La Nouvelle Héloïse* (1761).

When he came to a direct account of political theory in *The Social Contract* (1762), Rousseau developed the positive side of what he had presented negatively in the *Letter to M. d'Alembert*. Culture now appeared as the crucial element in democracy. The argument became snarled when Rousseau tried to explain how the General Will would express itself in a system of voting. But the confusion dissipated in the last chapter, where he revealed that what ultimately bound the citizens into a polity was a civil religion—not an otherworldly version of Christianity but an all-pervasive, Spartan style of patriotism. Patriots obeyed the General Will spontaneously. They wanted the common good because they were united by a common culture, the source of all morality. They would be virtuous by virtue of their citizenship and free because of their morals. In such a system, sanctions mattered less than education, and elections less than festivals.

That lesson was not lost on the French revolutionaries, who

were always parading through the streets in celebration of liberty and the civic virtues. When viewed from the present, Rousseau's civil religion can look menacing—a premonition of Nuremberg rallies—or familiar, an early version of football halftime shows. Either way, Rousseau seems to have put his finger on something important. It may seem strange that we mix flag-waving and football or that President Reagan should have synchronized his inauguration with the kickoff of the Super Bowl. I think Rousseau would have understood. Having traveled the enormous social distance that separated Genevan workshops from Parisian salons, he had learned to recognize symbolic forms of power. He expressed his insight in old fashioned moral rhetoric. But the moral of his story was really very modern, and it has yet to be assimilated, especially by those who remain convinced that power primarily comes out the barrel of a gun.

6

THE CRAZE FOR AMERICA:
CONDORCET AND BRISSOT

OPEN *Le Journal de Paris*, THE ONLY DAILY NEWSPAPER IN
FRANCE BEFORE THE REVOLUTION, AT ANY DATE FROM 1780
TO 1789, and you are bound to come across something about
America—not foreign news, which hardly existed, but American
themes that Parisians encountered in everyday life. The biggest hit
among the vaudeville theaters in 1786 is *L'Héroine américaine* at the
Ambigu-Comique. A rival troupe, Les Grands Danseurs du roi,
offers its own variation on the same theme, *Le Héro américain*, a
"pantomime in three acts, with dialogue, dances, music and combat," while, up market, the Comédie italienne is staging a *Ballet des
Quakers. D'Hirza ou les Illinois* is no longer playing on the boulevards,
but the connoisseur of "savage eloquence" can read Native American odes to nature in the "anecdotes" column of the paper. Better
yet, he can procure great chunks of Iroquois and Illinois translated
into Rousseauistic French in *Le Voyageur américain* and *Le Cultivateur
américain* available in bookshops throughout the Latin Quarter.

For a glimpse of a noble savage in the flesh, one can walk past
Lafayette's residence, where two Indians serve as houseboys.
Lafayette's himself, staring fiercely at the enemy at Yorktown, may
be admired in prints for sale all along the rue Saint-Jacques. Washington too may be purchased for a few pennies and pinned to one's

wall, alongside other stock figures—Virginia planters, Pennsylvania Quakers, Nantucket whalers—from prints and books. Franklin seems to be everywhere—as "Le Bonhomme Richard," the incarnation of common sense and the common man in everybody's almanac; as a statesman negotiating with the great under a coonskin cap at Versailles; and as a philosopher, sublimely bald, discoursing on electricity at the Academy of Sciences.

Franklin's successor, Thomas Jefferson, arrives in the wake of a wave of publications about the American Revolution. Jefferson's *Remarques sur la Virginie* may be sampled in the book review section of the *Journal,* along with extracts from the memoirs of several French veterans of the War of Independence and the occasional novel, like *Miss Mac Rea,* a revolutionary romance. Not that the new breed of American experts speaks with one voice. In letters to the editor, Thomas Paine disputes the accuracy of the New World depicted in the abbé Raynal's best-selling *Histoire philosophique et politique des établissements et du commerce des Européens dans les deux Indes,* and Filippo Mazzei polemicizes with the abbé Robin about Pennsylvania Quakers. But everyone has something to say: Saint John de Crèvecoeur as a *cultivateur américain,* the duc de La Rochefoucauld as a *bourgeois de New Haven,* Beaumarchais as *Beaumarchais l'américain,* for the subject is inexhaustible, even for hairdressers who advertise coiffures *à la Philadelphie* and *aux insurgents.*[1]

There is no mistaking the French fascination with America, but what did it mean? Different things to different people, of course, especially at the extremes on either end of the spectrum, where differences over the meaning of America corresponded to disputes about the fate of France. The case of Condorcet is particularly revealing in this respect because he observed the collapse of the Old Regime from a perspective that he considered American, yet he supported the government in the crisis of 1787–1788, while most of the American enthusiasts opposed it. Enthusiasm itself seemed dangerous to him. He represented the opposite extreme, reason, both pure and practical, in the struggle for control of the collective imagination.

Maric-Jean-Antoine-Nicolas Caritat, marquis de Condorcet, seems in retrospect to be the last of the *philosophes,* the incarnation of the Enlightenment in its final phase. As the successor to d'Alembert and a protégé of Voltaire and Turgot, he stood out both as a geometrician and as a crusader against all forms of injustice. He also passed as an expert on America. A friend of Franklin, Jefferson, and Lafayette, he could claim to be an American himself. In 1785 he was made an honorary citizen of *"New Haven dans la Nouvelle Yorck,"* as the *Journal de Paris* reported, coping as best it could with the exotic geography.[2] Condorcet took his Americanization seriously. He signed his most important prerevolutionary pamphlets as *"un bourgeois de New-Haven," "un citoyen des États-Unis,"* and *"un républicain."* He was passionately pro-American. But his passion was for reason.

Where other Frenchmen peopled their American fantasies with noble savages and sturdy yeomen, Condorcet saw a problem of applied mathematics. He claimed that the theory of probability developed in his *Essai sur l'application de l'analyse à la probabilité des décisions rendues à la pluralité des voix* (1785) provided the answer to the question of how to organize elections in the new republic, which in turn could serve as a model for political systems everywhere.[3] America could teach Europeans to ignore history and to derive politics from abstract principles of justice and natural rights. By applying reason, "which never deceives," enlightened citizens could develop a new "science of legislation." In fact, by following the American example, they could produce a whole new science of society, which would improve endlessly in response to the endless expansion of human knowledge.[4]

It was therefore in his capacity as an American and as a participant in polemics about the United States that Condorcet first developed his theory of progress, long before the publication of his famous *Esquisse d'un tableau historique des progrès de l'esprit humain* in 1795. That the concept of progress should be connected by some elective affinity to an American way of life may not seem surprising today, at least not to progressively minded Americans, but there was nothing self-evident about the connection to eighteenth-century Frenchmen. On the contrary, they liked to imagine the Americans as primitives, who frequently took to the woods in order to escape civilization and live close to nature, with the Indians.[5] Condorcet himself did not picture the Americans as sophisticates. Like his contemporaries, he celebrated their simplicity and equality in contrast with the social divisions that produced so much injustice in France. But he imagined them as philosophers, so given over to ratiocination in their rustic retreats that they would soon double the general stock of knowledge:

> America offers the prospect of a vast land populated by several million men who, thanks to their education, have been made immune to prejudice and inclined to study and reflection. No distinction of rank or pull of ambition can deter these men from the natural desire to perfect their minds, to apply their intelligence to useful research, to aspire to the glory that comes with great works and discoveries. Nothing there keeps part of the human race in an abject state, condemned to stupidity and destitution. There is therefore reason to hope that by producing as many men devoted to the increase of knowledge as in all of Europe, America will in a few generations double the mass of knowledge and the speed of its accumulation. This progress will take place equally in the useful arts and the speculative sciences.[6]

In this fantasy, titled *De l'influence de la révolution d'Amérique sur l'Europe* (1786) and dedicated to Lafayette, Condorcet piled one abstract proposition on top of another, as if he were deducing theorems in geometry. None of them bore much relation to the actual country across the Atlantic, but that did not matter, because America for Condorcet was a mental experiment. Having never traveled far from Paris, except for one visit to Voltaire's estate near Geneva, he remained free to design the country he wanted in his imagination. He therefore made America into the antithesis of everything he deplored in France. It enjoyed social equality, equitable and moderate taxation, free trade, and an unrestricted press. Americans were so dedicated to religious freedom that they made tolerance their "dearest dogma," they were so committed to liberty that they would soon abolish slavery, they were so peace-loving that they would produce an end to warfare in Europe by the sheer force of their example, and they were so unshakeably rational that they would contribute more than anyone else to "the perfectability of the human species."[7]

Of course many other Frenchmen used America as a screen on which to project similar programs for reform in France. One can see what set Condorcet's fantasy apart from the standard fare by considering *Lettres d'un cultivateur américain* (1784) by Hector Saint John de Crèvecoeur, probably the most popular of all the books on America except for the *Histoire philosophique* of the abbé Raynal. Crèvecoeur passed as a *sauvage américain* in the fashionable salons of Paris, although he actually came from the minor nobility of Normandy.[8] Having left to seek his fortune in the New World at the age of nineteen, he had hacked two farms out of the wilderness, had himself naturalized, married an American woman, and recorded the transformation of his life in a kind of journal, where he became the first to ask the question, What is an American? He answered it with a combination of personal observation and Enlightenment philosophy acquired from a reading of Raynal, and he did so in homespun English, which had enough appeal, when he submitted it to a London publisher, to be published as *Letters from an American Farmer* in 1782. Back in France, Crèvecoeur was taken up by the comtesse d'Houdetot and her circle, notably the lawyer-*littérateur* G.-J.-B. Target and the poet J.-F. de Saint-Lambert, who helped him "translate" his English into overheated, Rousseauistic French, adding a heavy dose of virtuous Quakers and eloquent Indians. By subtracting, so to speak, the English from the French edition, which was twice as long, one can see how American themes were transformed through French *sensiblerie*.

One example should suffice. In the English *Letters,* Crèvecoeur observes that because they lived close to nature, Americans favored a "natural" religion in place of an established church. In the French *Lettres,* this religion turned into a version of the ecstatic deism preached by Rousseau's Savoyard vicar. A two-page passage, which consisted mainly of observations on the habits of birds in the English, became a six-page hymn to nature in the French. The Frenchified American farmer sings along with the birds, prays in his fields, and retires to a "temple of greenery," where he communes with nature: ". . . Oh! sweet breath of Nature, thou comest, carried on the wings of zephirs; already thy reason speaks through the leaves that surround me everywhere." And thus edified, he indoctrinates his children in a sentimental civil religion: "I lead them into the fields, I teach them to think, to feel as I do; I plant in their tender hearts the first principles of universal morality, of probity, rectitude, truth, humanity, obedience to the law. . . . I have composed for them a prayer to God under the name of Father of Farmers."[9]

This was precisely the kind of enthusiasm that set Condorcet's teeth on edge. Having worn white dresses in honor of the Virgin until the age of at least eight and then suffered through spiritual exercises in a Jesuit school, he had contracted a fierce case of anticlericalism and felt no sympathy for religion of any kind, whether Catholic, Quaker, or Rousseauian. He had enlisted in Voltaire's church—that is, in the battle against *l'infâme,* or religious persecution, and for the rights of man. He aligned himself with the older generation of *philosophes,* especially d'Alembert, who treated him as a son, and Turgot, who recruited him for the cause of enlightened reform. Condorcet saw America as the embodiment of that cause, and he made his American tracts into manifestos for reform in France: for religious toleration (that is, the granting of civil rights to Protestants), the repeal of the *corvée* (forced labor by peasants on royal roads), freedom of trade (by abolishing the regulation of grain prices, internal tariffs, and guilds), and the creation of an equitable taxation system (by means of a land tax, which would fall equally on all proprietors and would be regulated by elected assemblies). All these themes appeared in pamphlets that Condorcet wrote as an American after discussing politics with Americans—not rhapsodic farmers of the Crèvecoeur variety but *philosophes* from the American Philosophical Society: Benjamin Franklin and Thomas Jefferson.

Many of the discussions took place in the Parisian *hôtels* of two distinguished widows, Mme. Helvétius and Mme. d'Enville. Insofar as these informal get-togethers had a political agenda, it was set by Turgot, a close friend of both ladies, who nursed him after the collapse of his ministry and his health in 1776. Turgot had opposed France's intervention in the American war, mainly (and quite rightly) on financial grounds, but he supported the American cause wholeheartedly. In an essay of 1778 he celebrated it as "the hope of the human race" and identified it with his own reform program.[10] After his death, in 1781, that program continued to inspire the liberal aristocrats of the d'Enville circle, notably Lafayette; Mme. d'Enville's son, the duc de La Rochefoucauld d'Enville; and her nephew, the marquis de La Rochefoucauld-Liancourt. In frequenting that circle, Condorcet drifted increasingly away from pure mathematics and toward political arithmetic, the politics that he advocated as a *bourgeois de New Haven* and that corresponded with many of the reforms instituted during the first two years of the French Revolution. Those were the years of Lafayette.[11] But to reach Lafayette in the salon of the Hôtel d'Enville, one had to walk past Houdon's bust of Condorcet, stationed on a marble table.[12]

The radical rationalism of the d'Enville circle is worthy of note because it represents one extreme in the complex ideological landscape of prerevolutionary Paris. The salon of Mme. d'Houdetot stood for another: sentimental Rousseauism, which also provided fuel for the American craze in Paris. Whereas Mme. d'Enville had mothered Turgot, Mme. d'Houdetot had captivated Rousseau, who saw her as the incarnation of his Julie in *La Nouvelle Héloïse*. And while Mme. d'Enville played hostess to Jefferson, Mme. d'Houdetot sponsored Crèvecoeur, a less exalted but more appealing figure: "Proud of possessing an American savage, she wanted to mold him and launch him in high society."[13] That was the judgment of Jacques-Pierre Brissot, the future leader of the Girondist party in the French Revolution, who also regarded Crèvecoeur as a "man of nature" and tried to enlist him, at a lower level of society, in another activity that they took to be American, the conquest of public opinion.[14]

Crèvecoeur had already conquered a large segment of the reading public in 1784 with his spectacularly successful *Lettres d'un cultivateur américain*. At that time Brissot was struggling to establish himself as a man of letters among a colony of French expatriates in London. He published a journal in which he championed various radical causes, including everything American, having embraced America as "the new fatherland that I had adopted in my heart."[15] This conversion resulted from a reading of Crèvecoeur. In a rapturous review of the *Lettres d'un cultivateur américain,* Brissot announced that he had now learned that everything dreamed of in his fondest fantasies actually existed in a republic located on the other side of the ocean, in the bosom of nature, and at a safe distance from the corrupting effects of European civilization: "Why did Rousseau not live longer? He would have read M. de St. John and would have been consoled by seeing the realization of those dreams that his enemies have ridiculed so relentlessly. This fact will be the consolation of *philosophes* today whose sublime ideas are often subjected to the same scorn."[16]

What might some of this Americanized Rousseauism produce if

it were injected into the body politic of France? Brissot began to
play with this idea in 1786. Having returned to Paris and survived
two disastrous months in the Bastille, he sought out Crèvecoeur
and soon became bound to him by "the most tender friendship and
a great affinity of sentiments."[17] He was also closely attached to two
other radical Rousseauists: Étienne Clavière, a financier who had
settled in Paris after an unsuccessful attempt at organizing a revolution in his native Geneva in 1782, and Nicolas Bergasse, a lawyer
who mixed revolutionary speculation with pseudoscience as
France's leading champion of mesmerism. On January 2, 1787,
Brissot, Crèvecoeur, Clavière, and Bergasse founded an association
designed to promote closer relations between the United States
and France, the Gallo-American Society.

Although the Gallo-Americans planned to establish branches
throughout both countries and to stimulate discussion of all things
American by means of publications and correspondence, their projects never came to much. They met regularly every week for nearly
four months but suspended their activities when they became
caught up in events connected with the prerevolutionary crisis of
1787. When read at a distance of two hundred years, the minutes
of their meetings present a bewildering jumble of topics: a life
insurance scheme, a campaign against adultery, general philan-
thropy, and the creation of a free port at Honfleur.[18] What did these
causes have to do with one another and with the United States?
They concerned various enterprises of the society's members:
Clavière's speculations on the Bourse, Bergasse's defense of his
friend Guillaume Kornmann in an adultery trial, Brissot's involve-
ment in humanitarian schemes of the duc d'Orléans, and Crèvecoeur's attempts to promote the trade of his native Normandy. But
what held them together and made them appropriate topics for discussion in the minds of the Gallo-Americans was their connection
with political morality or the austere republican virtues that they

associated with the United States. As they equated America with the cause of humanity and the pursuit of happiness, nearly anything sufficiently moral could qualify as American. Thus, when they debated the purpose of the society, the members resolved that ". . . although its ostensible and immediate object is the interest of France and the United States, it nevertheless includes the happiness of humanity as part of its general goal."[19]

Vague as it sounds, this moralizing contributed powerfully to the radicalization of public opinion on the eve of the Revolution. It injected a dose of militant Rousseauism into the French fantasies about homespun farmers and Quakers, and it gave a polemical edge to what was originally little more than a fashion. The polemics were stirred up by a series of books and pamphlets that the Gallo-Americans published between 1786 and 1788. The two works most closely associated with the society were *De la France et des États-Unis* by Brissot and Clavière and the 1787 edition of Crèvecoeur's *Lettres d'un cultivateur américain.*

Although ostensibly a treatise on commerce, *De la France et des États-Unis* reads like a political tract. France should export wool rather than silk textiles and copper rather than silver utensils to America, Brissot and Clavière argued, because luxury goods were incompatible with republicanism: "People governed by a free constitution are necessarily grave and reflective. In the articles of everyday life, they prefer things that are good to things that are brilliant, solid things to things valued merely because they happen to be in style. As long as the free Americans [the Gallo-Americans insisted on terms like "free Americans" and "free America" to distinguish the United States from the colonial territories of the New World] benefit from their excellent constitution, they will prefer to dress themselves in woolens rather than fancier materials."[20]

From woolens it was but a small step to the rights of man, social equality, public happiness, the social contract, and the right of rev-

olution, concepts that Brissot and Clavière sprinkled freely through
their account of tariffs, shipping, and the balance of trade.[21]

Crèvecoeur did the same in the new volume that he added to his
Lettres d'un cultivateur américain in 1787. While filling the volume
with all sorts of practical information about opportunities for
expanding the commerce between France and the United States, he
made America seem more mythical than ever. To the themes of
domestic simplicity and arcadian virtue, he now added a utopian
element. One chapter described a group of Europeans who con-
gregated in a country tavern in order to plan a new community,
"Socialburg." One after another, each testified to the evils that had
driven him out of Europe: monarchical wars, religious persecution, commercialization, and "the oppressive tyranny of our mano-
rial lords." Then they drew up a social contract, which laid down
the principles of the polity they were creating. It would be based on
agrarian virtues—"Honor the plow"—on equality—"Look upon
all [men] as equal by birth,"—on toleration and a deistic civil religion—". . . The foundation of society must be the cult we owe to
the Supreme Being, the father of farmers"—on the spirit of "fra-
ternal union,"—and on something like a General Will, which
would militate against any form of inequality, especially in taxation:
"All will be required to make the same payments, according to laws
passed in the name of all."[22] In another chapter, set in Ireland, a
group of peasant "Notables" declared the feudal regime so brutal
that they considered the social contract broken. They contemplated
rising in revolt and massacring the local aristocracy, but finally
decided to emigrate to America, where they founded another egalitarian community like Socialburg.[23] As the book was published a
few weeks after the Assembly of Notables began debating reforms
in France, it looked even more suspicious than the edition of 1784,
which the censor refused to pass and which was received, when it
finally appeared with a tacit permission, as an attack on "political

slavery and moral corruption," according to a review in the *Mercure.*[24]

The most outspoken of all the Gallo-American publications was a short book by Brissot, *Examen critique des voyages dans l'Amérique septentrionale de M. le marquis de Chastellux.* Although it added no new ideas to the debate about America, it changed the tone, because it denounced the marquis de Chastellux as a decadent aristocrat and his account of his travels in the United States as a "poison," the product of a desiccated soul.[25] In fact Chastellux had treated the United States sympathetically and had merely tossed off a few witticisms at the expense of Quakers and other stock figures in the fantasies of the French. As a friend of Voltaire and a partisan of the physiocrats he favored progressive causes. And as a well-known member of the Académie française he knew how to turn a phrase. But that was the problem in Brissot's view: Chastellux was witty, wit was an aristocratic weapon, and the blue-blooded academician had turned it on the very Americans who were most innocent and most virtuous, according to Crèvecoeur—Quakers, blacks, and the common people.

To judge from the *Examen,* the public would think that Chastellux and Crèvecoeur had engaged in a major debate about the nature of society, and sensitive readers would know where to find the truth: "Even if I did not know M. de C. [Crèvecoeur], even if I had not read his soul a hundred times, I would be able to form a judgment merely by reading your two books. The soul alone dictated his. Yours proves that you have a great deal of wit, but it is with the soul that one must judge republicans, men of pure morals, and such are the Quakers."[26]

By suggesting that African Americans were inferior to whites, Chastellux had failed to heed the call of nature, "that good mother who wants us all to be equal, free, and happy." And by denigrating the American common people, he had reinforced the subjugation of the underprivileged everywhere: "The dignity of man consists in his liberty, in his equality before the law, in his independence, in his subordination only to those laws to which he has given his consent, in the control he exercises over those to whom he has confided his authority. . . . I say that man in our societies does not have that dignity."[27]

This was propaganda aimed at France. When he wrote it, Brissot was consumed with enthusiasm for everything American, but he had never set foot in the United States, and he took as his target a gentleman-*philosophe* who had fought in the American Revolution and was a good friend of George Washington's.

By this time the debate about America was polarizing around two positions, which had more to do with style than substance: Rousseauian enthusiasm versus Enlightenment rationalism. Brissot and Clavière represented such an extreme version of the former that moderate periodicals such as the *Mercure* and the *Journal de Paris* refused to review their works and to publish their letters to the editor. It was a conspiracy of silence, Brissot later wrote: "The *Journal de Paris,* among others, had always sold out to men in power, those with pull, the little despots of literature. . . ."[28] But to established writers, particularly those from the Académie française, like Jean-François de La Harpe, Brissot was ". . . one of those effected madmen, the extravagant souls who have made themselves into the monkeys of Jean-Jacques Rousseau and who, by repeating words like virtue and humanity over and over again, think they are as eloquent as he was."[29]

La Harpe consigned his attack on Brissot's *Examen*—"revolting, both by its bitterness and its grossness"[30]—to his privately circulated *Correspondance littéraire.* But the *Journal de Paris* did not entirely ignore the polemics stirred up by the book. In November and December 1786 it printed an exchange of letters that further helped to define the issues dividing the two camps. The first letter, signed

"Ferri," came from Filippo Mazzei, a Tuscan who had emigrated to Virginia, where he became a friend and neighbor of Thomas Jefferson's, and then settled in Jefferson's entourage in Paris.[31] Not only did Mazzei attack Brissot and defend Chastellux, but he also struck at the French infatuation with American Quakers, whom he termed *Jésuites Protestants*. They were shrewd merchants, not utopian idealists, Mazzei claimed, and he cited authorities like Jefferson and Thomas Paine in support of his argument. The rebuttal came in a letter from yet another authority, the abbé Charles-César Robin, who had served as chaplain to Rochambeau's troops and also had published a travel book about America. The Quakers were every bit as warmhearted, simple, and virtuous as they were reputed to be, Robin testified, although he did not have anything good to say about Brissot. Mazzei then backed away from an open quarrel by answering that Quakers were not bad, just no better than anyone else and particularly fond of making money. For an accurate picture of America, French readers should consult yet another book: "An eloquent and philosophical American will soon publish a work about the United States of America in which he will refute the innumerable errors spread about by those who have treated the same subject as if it were a romance composed by rhetoricians. The precise history that he will give of the Quakers will make it impossible for anyone to believe any more in the utopia of Penn."[32]

This book was the *Recherches historiques et politiques sur les États-Unis de l'Amérique septentrionale,* a four-tome treatise by the same Filippo Mazzei. It was a key work in the French debates about the United States because it marked the point at which rationalism confronted Rousseauism and the Gallo-American myth was challenged by Americans of a very different kidney, men like Thomas Jefferson and his friend the *bourgeois de New Haven,* Condorcet.

Jefferson worried about the unrealistic views of America held in France. He attributed them to the influence of literary men like

Raynal and Mably, who perpetrated wild ideas about the state of nature along with potentially damaging misinformation about the effectiveness of the state governments and the conditions of trade. When J.-N. Demeunier asked for help on his article about the United States for the *Encyclopédie méthodique*. Jefferson spent many hours weeding out inaccuracies. Even so, the article retained far too much fantasy for Jefferson's taste: "He has left in a great deal of the abbé Raynal, that is to say a great deal of falsehood."[33] Mazzei intended his *Recherches historiques* to be an antidote to such romanticizing. In a letter to James Madison, he explained its origins as follows: "Abbé Raynal had for a long time been getting on my nerves, and abbé de Mably's *Observations* [*Observations sur le gouvernement et les lois des États-Unis d'Amérique*, 1784] on our governments made my blood boil as soon as I saw it and heard it had made a bad impression. . . . I began a thorough-going refutation. . . . The greatest mathematician and most vigorous writer in France, the marquis de Condorcet, said that I did the two abbés too much honor by making them the 'heroes of my poem.' The Duke de La Rochefoucauld laughed at his designation, but shared his sentiment."[34]

Mazzei's book turned into a virtual encyclopedia of information about America, much of it supplied by Jefferson and worked over by Condorcet, who vetted the translation into French and added two essays of his own, the *Lettres d'un bourgeois de New-Haven* and *De l'influence de la révolution d'Amérique sur l'Europe*. In a sense, therefore, the *Recherches historiques* was a collective work that represented the America championed not merely by Jefferson but by all his friends from the Hôtel d'Enville, above all Condorcet.

It also operated as a direct assault on the America imagined by the enthusiasts of Crèvecoeur. Like Benjamin Franklin before him, Jefferson often received letters from Frenchmen who were so besotted with the American myth that they wanted to jump on the next boat for Boston. One of Crèvecoeur's readers wrote rapturously: "You are made to legislate for us, because for us you are men from the Golden Age. . . . Ah, Monsieur, your land is the promised land. . . . How happy would I be to exist in such a fine country, where I would be a man instead of a slave as I am here."[35] Jefferson worried that such sentiments might provoke a wave of misguided immigrants. Mazzei tried to counter them by warning that Crève-coeur's *Lettres* did not provide an accurate picture of American life and that many Frenchmen had acquired "the most far-fetched ideas by reading that book."[36]

Those remarks provoked another round of polemics in 1788. Brissot fulminated against Mazzei in three articles printed by Mirabeau in his *L'Analyse des papiers anglois,* a periodical that championed the favorite themes of the Gallo-Americans. Brissot went over all of them once more, from the vices of luxury to the virtues of Quakerism, but he added nothing except vehemence to the debate: "To attack such a worthy person [as Crèvecoeur] is to insult talent, the human race, sound morals, France, and the American republics; it is to warrant excommunication from them."[37] Condorcet took charge of Mazzei's defense. In a letter to the *Journal de Paris,* he accused Brissot of being "carried away by enthusiasm" in contrast with Mazzei, who took a better-informed and more balanced view of the United States. Condorcet revealed that Jefferson thought so highly of Mazzei's warning against ill-considered immigration that he had had extra copies of the relevant chapter of the *Recherches historiques* printed for distribution to potential immigrants. Writing as an insider from Jefferson's circle, Condorcet argued for reason and moderation in comparing the United States with Europe: "I suspect that he [Mazzei] believes, like M. Franklin and M. Jefferson, like many other Americans, that there exists in Europe, and even in European monarchies, some great talent, great knowledge, and great virtues. I suspect that he does not look upon all Europeans as monsters and Americans as angels."[38]

By this time the debate about America had become swallowed up in the agitation over the fall of the Old Regime in France. Most of the polemicists threw themselves into the campaign for the Estates General, taking up positions that would be identified with the "patriot" party or what would soon be known as the Left. They did not abandon their commitment to American issues, however. Many of them patched up their differences and drew together in an association that succeeded the Gallo-American Society, the French Society of the Friends of the Blacks, which was devoted to a cause that united nearly all friends of America—namely, the abolition of the slave trade. Brissot founded the Society on February 19, 1788; Clavière acted as its first president; Condorcet later took over its direction; and by early 1789 it had 141 members, including Crève-coeur (a corresponding member because he was then the French consul in New York), Bergasse, Lafayette, Mazzei, the duc de La Rochefoucauld, and Jefferson's secretary, William Short (evidently Jefferson felt his official status as representative of the United States made it inappropriate for him to join).[39]

The rush of events produced many realignments among the allies and enemies from the American polemics of the 1780s. What set Condorcet apart through them all was not identification with a party—not even the Girondists, with whom he was condemned in 1793—but adherence to reason. He always thought for himself and expounded his position rationally, even in the most heated moments of conflict. During the so-called prerevolution of 1787–1788, when nearly all the participants in the American debates turned against the government—Mazzei, Lafayette, and La Rochefoucauld as well as Brissot, Clavière, and Bergasse—he sup-ported it. It was not that he was more conservative than they—on the contrary, he took a more extreme position than most of them on issues such as tax reform and representative assemblies, not to mention the rights of women and the campaign against slavery—

but he calculated that the reforms proposed by the Calonne and Brienne ministries represented the most coherent program for fundamental change, and he distrusted the aristocratic tendency of the antigovernment agitators in the parlements, including some of the fire-eaters known as "Americans."[40]

Condorcet's independent stand on political issues produced some severe tension between him and his closest friends, notably Lafayette and La Rochefoucauld, in 1788.[41] But they united again in support of the revolution of 1789, and Condorcet praised Lafayette fulsomely in a eulogy of Franklin before the Academy of Sciences in 1790, taking care, as always, to reserve his strongest praise for reason as opposed to enthusiasm.[42] In the following year, however, Lafayette emerged as the leader of the new Right. He commanded the massacre of the Champ-de-Mars and founded the reactionary Feuillant Club, while Condorcet took up republicanism in the company of his old enemy, Jacques-Pierre Brissot, among the Jacobins. This split finally brought an end to the friendships that had flourished in the Hôtel d'Enville.[43] The old duchess closed her doors to Condorcet. His bust disappeared into a storeroom and did not see the light of day again until it arrived at the American Philosophical Society. By then Condorcet had followed Brissot and the Girondists into defeat and death, and Jefferson, drawing up "a course of reading," had listed his last work, the *Esquisse d'un tableau historique des progrès de l'esprit humain,* as a classic, along with Locke's *Essay concerning Human Understanding* and Smith's *Wealth of Nations.* "Of Condorcet's [*Esquisse*] I need say nothing. Every thing of his is of established reputation."[44]

THE PURSUIT OF PROFIT: ROUSSEAUISM ON THE BOURSE

"Business is business." Like "War is war" and "art for art's sake," the refrain echoes across the centuries with a finality that seems to put everything in place. But what precisely was the place of business, or rather finance, in prerevolutionary France? I should like to argue that finance, politics, and ideology intermingled in ways that defy the conventional dividing lines of history and that Rousseauism belonged to the scramble for power and lucre on what would seem to be a most unlikely site, the Parisian Bourse. Speculation on the Bourse fed directly into sedition against the government, as one can see by examining the careers of a financier, Étienne Clavière, and a pamphleteer, Jacques-Pierre Brissot, in the years 1785–87.[1]

When the police turned Brissot out of the Bastille on September 10, 1784, he was a ruined man. He had lost everything he owned in a series of disastrous publishing ventures. His debts came to 20,000 to 30,000 livres, the equivalent of a lifetime's wages for a skilled laborer. He had a wife and baby to support and no job, no home, no prospects of employment. For a few months in the winter of 1784–1785, he found refuge in the house of his mother-in-law, the widow of a merchant in Boulogne. Then he settled in Paris, where Filippo Mazzei was appalled to find the family (a second child was born in March 1786) crammed into two rooms and dressed "in rags." But there was no getting around it: Brissot's dream of winning a respectable place in the Republic of Letters had ended in Grub Street. He had become a hack, living on literary odd jobs and the hope that something might turn up.[2]

That something was Étienne Clavière. Clavière had been run out of Geneva for siding with the radical Représentants during the municipal revolution of 1782. He had toyed for a while with the idea of founding a colony of republican watchmakers in Waterford, Ireland, and finally had settled in Paris in order to play the stock market.

His account books, now in the Archives Nationales, show that he was a wealthy man. He had invested 1,293,770 livres in annuities (*rentes viagères*), which brought in 116,785 livres a year; and he supplemented this basic income with three other sources of revenue: bonds worth 457,000 livres, a great deal of stock[3] whose value was not specified, and additional *rentes* that paid 13,455 livres annually. Instead of letting the income accumulate, Clavière speculated with it. He put money on anything that fired his imagination—utopian colonies, the tea trade, a "splendid secret for [producing] vinegar," a secret process for refining cotton, glass manufacturing, Parisian real estate, a country house near Surène worth 64,600 livres, distilling, schemes for insurance and water supply companies, and paintings, including some by Rembrandt, Rubens, and Van Dyck. Clavière combined fervent idealism with a shrewd business sense. He was an adventurer, a gambler in a variety of political and financial projects, who threw himself into the Revolution and took his own life when he realized that he had lost his greatest gamble, the fight against the Robespierrists. In the 1780s he went down in the files of the secret police as a powerful personality at the Bourse: "He is a man with a dark turn of mind, good at calculating but fond of luxury. He is an excellent speaker, but he is feared and hated."[4]

Clavière also invested heavily in Brissot. A cynic could argue that in the long run the speculation paid off because Brissot cleared a way for Clavière to take over the Finance Ministry in 1792. But there is no reason to doubt that the two future Girondins were united by a genuine friendship in the 1780s. According to his memoirs, Brissot looked upon Clavière, who was his senior by nineteen years, as a *"sage mentor,"* a "veritable father," who saved him from bankruptcy out of sheer altruism.[5] Of course the memoirs should be read with care; they contain errors and distortions on almost every page, as one might expect from a man writing in the shadow of the guillotine. To form a more precise idea of Clavière's rescue operation and of the interpenetration of finance and ideology, one can consult his financial papers, which were impounded after his arrest on June 2, 1793.

The papers, mostly scribbled notes and incomplete account books, contain little information for the period before 1786. By then Clavière had loaned Brissot 10,000 livres to cover his most pressing debts, and Brissot had worked out an arrangement with his publisher that covered the bulk of his other liabilities. But he still had no regular income—except what he drew from Clavière. Clavière's "cashbox book" shows he paid Brissot 3,383-4-0 livres between December 1785 and November 1786. Of this, 1,384 livres represented straightforward cash payments, enough to support a family for a year, and the remainder concerned letters of credit from others that Clavière cashed for Brissot. In short, Clavière acted as Brissot's banker.[6]

On November 3, 1786, Clavière formalized this situation by giving Brissot an account number, 73, which from then on he entered in the left margin of his "journal of accounts" as he recorded credits and debits. He seems to have paid out cash to Brissot as the need arose, noting the sums in a separate account book, and then entered several payments together in the journal as a single debit against Brissot's account. Thus, for example, the journal entries for June 20, 1788:

20 June: Debit cash and credit J.-J. Clavière [Étienne Clavière's brother and business associate] for the following items, which he paid on my behalf: 200 livres to Warville [Brissot, who had added "de Warville" to his surname]; 200 livres to Warville, 300 livres to Warville, 150 livres to the same. . . .

20 June: Debit Brissot de Warville and credit cash for the following sums paid to him:

300	livres that I paid him on May 14
400	livres from J.-J. Clavière on the 20th
300	livres ditto on the 24th
120	livres from me on the 27th
200	livres for his note to the credit of Verguin on the 10th of this month
277	ditto to Gally
900	livres ditto to Brabant on the 30th of last month
240	livres paid to his wife on the 10th of last month
78	livres ditto to his brother on the 16th of last month
96	livres my bill of exchange on Th. and Fc. Cazenove payment to the bearer at [a discount of] 4 livres 14 sols
312	livres ditto at 12 livres 19 sols
1500	livres my note on J.-J. Clavière, which I reimbursed
179	livres his note to the credit of Lejay on the 10th of this month
4902	[total]

By January 30, 1789, when the journal ends, Brissot had received 24,653-11-0 from Clavière and had deposited only 20,982-10-0, which came in large part from further loans, provided by family and friends.

Brissot drew on Clavière so constantly and repaid him so rarely that it would be misleading to regard the transactions as analogous to those of a modern bank account. Clavière probably meant to help a friend in distress and to do so systematically rather than piecemeal, as he had done before November 1786. But the account had another purpose, which Clavière indicated in its first entry: Brissot had opened the account with a deposit of 2,000 livres (probably a loan from his mother-in-law) "to be used in speculations for his account." Those speculations can be reconstructed, at least in part, from Clavière's papers, and they are worth studying, because they lead to the heart of the operations on the Bourse at one of the most explosive moments in French history.

Clavière's interventions on the Bourse for Brissot took the form of *marchés à prime,* an eighteenth-century version of modern stock transactions involving options to buy or sell shares at a future date. The *prime,* or premium, was a payment made for the privilege to opt out of a sale on the agreed date if the value of the shares had changed disadvantageously, in which case only the *prime* would be forfeited. It was a relatively safe version of the *marché à terme,* in which *haussiers,* or bull speculators, gambled on futures against *baissiers,* or bear speculators, without an escape clause.[7]

Clavière's first speculation for Brissot provides a good example of a bear type of *marché à prime.* On December 5, 1786, Clavière debited Brissot's account for a *prime* of 1,580 livres to cover the sale of 100 shares of the Banque de Saint-Charles to the Genevan banker Jacques Achard, who promised to buy them at 600 livres a share on December 31, 1787. For some reason, the speculation was settled early, on August 20, 1787. At that time Clavière credited 5,427 livres to Brissot's account, a thumping profit, because Achard had to pay the difference between the agreed price of 64,000 livres and the current selling price of 58,500 livres. Clavière had served Brissot well and took a commission of 73 livres.

Clavière's other speculations for Brissot concerned three *marchés à prime* on shares of the Compagnie des assurances contre les incendies and the Compagnie des assurances contre la vie. The first, which involved Brissot in a transaction with the notorious stock-jobber C.-L.-J. Baroud, produced a loss of 1,500 livres. The results of the other two cannot be determined because they took place in 1788, when the entries in Clavière's journal become so sparse that it is impossible to follow transactions in detail. But despite its spottiness, the evidence demonstrates that Brissot depended heavily on Clavière's operations on the Bourse to extricate himself from an overwhelming burden of debt. Brissot gambled with capital that he did not possess on stocks that he never saw. It was a dangerous business, but not nearly so dangerous as Clavière's own speculations, which were audacious enough to rock the entire Bourse.

The Bourse had not amounted to much during the half century after its establishment in the rue Vivienne opposite the stables of the duc d'Orléans in 1724. It merely provided Parisians with a place where they could buy and sell bills of exchange and shares in a half dozen joint stock companies for a few hours every morning before they settled down to their midday meal. But in the 1780s the Bourse erupted in a speculative mania, which spilled over into the cafés of the Palais-Royal, accompanied by occasional brawls and violent polemics conducted through pamphlets. Because stock stood for invisible assets—wealth located in the East Indies or profits tied up in projects for supplying Parisians with water or life insurance—it could easily be inflated: hence the pejorative term *agioteurs* for jobbers who added fictitious value to stock by concerted buying and whisper campaigns about fat dividends about to be declared or profitable assets about to be acquired. As a *baissier,* Clavière played by the opposite strategy. He staked hundreds of thousands of livres on bets that stock would fall, and when he got a chance, he precipitated falls by exposing inflated stock. Having contracted to sell shares, which he did not own, at a high price on a future date, he could buy them at a low price just before that date and pocket the difference.

The whole operation turned on the perceived value of shares—

that is, on public opinion. By 1786 this "public" no longer consisted of a few insider traders in the rue Vivienne. The speculative fever had spread through the moneyed classes even further than in the giddiest days of Law's system. Wild swings in the value of stock were announced every day in the *Journal de Paris* and discussed at length in clandestine gazettes, such as the *Mémoires secrets pour servir à l'histoire de la République des Lettres en France* and the *Correspondance littéraire* of J. H. Meister. Speculators like Clavière needed publi cists like Brissot. Both men occupied a strategic position in terri tory where the Bourse and the Republic of Letters intersected.

The collaboration between Clavière and Brissot went back to 1782, when they met in the Prussian principality of Neuchâtel, Switzerland. Clavière had arrived there as a refugee from the aborted Genevan revolution, Brissot as a fledgling *philosophe* in search of a Swiss publisher. Clavière needed a propagandist for his cause, Brissot had a ready pen, and the result was *Le Philadelphien à Genève,* a violent diatribe against Clavière's enemies in the aristro cratic Négatif party, which Brissot wrote in the person of an Amer ican revolutionary who had somehow strayed into Genevan politics and immediately recognized Clavière's Représentants as fellow spirits. As a "Philadelphian," Brissot proclaimed the austere moral ity of the Représentants to be the essence of genuine republican ism, and he cited the works of Rousseau, *The Social Contract* above all, as justification for everything they had done to overthrow the tyranny of the corrupt Négatifs.[8]

By 1784 circumstances had changed. Having rescued Brissot from bankruptcy, Clavière confided to his publisher that they had to depend on "whatever his pen can turn out" for reimbursement.[9] The collaborative character of this writing is suggested by one of Clavière's letters to Brissot in 1783: "Come. We will have a chat, and you will take notes. You will do me some good, and perhaps I will do the same for you."[10] Brissot himself described their collab oration in his memoirs: "Clavière, as I have already observed, had an inexhaustible stock of ideas, ideas that were grand and well suited to captivate minds; but he lacked the ability to express them effectively. He had not mastered the art of analysis; there was no order in his thoughts, no clarity in his style. He was a superior thinker, but he required someone else to write for him."[11]

The memoirs, however, say very little about the mutual interests of Brissot and Clavière on the Bourse. Brissot's autobiographical *Réponse de Jacques-Pierre Brissot à tous les libellistes qui ont attaqué et attaquent sa vie passée* (1791) says even less—one sentence, to be exact: "I will skip over the study I devoted to finance, in which I was instructed by my profound friend [Clavière], and a few works that I published in this domain."[12] In fact these "few works" were the most important works to come from Brissot's pen between the time of his release from the Bastille and the outbreak of the Revolution. They were his way of repaying Clavière for saving him from bankruptcy and supporting his family.

Brissot's role as Clavière's pamphleteer has never been fully appreciated, because most of the pamphlets appeared under the name of Mirabeau. In fact a whole stable of writers, including Brissot, du Pont de Nemours, and A.-J. Gorsas, worked with Mirabeau, who supplied rhetorical flourishes and a name that attracted attention. Clavière coordinated their work with the speculations of the *baissiers,* a group made up of Protestants, Genevans, and political radicals like Benjamin Panchaud, Théophile Casenove, and Étienne Delessert. The result was a series of polemical works that led straight from the conflicts on the Bourse in 1785 to the struggle for power during the prerevolution of 1787–88:

De la Caisse d'Escompte. Par le comte de Mirabeau (1785)

De la Banque d'Espagne, dite de Saint-Charles. Par le comte de Mirabeau (1785)

Lettre du comte de Mirabeau à M. le Couteulx de la Noraye, sur la Banque de Saint-Charles & sur la Caisse d'Escompte (1785)

Sur les actions de la Compagnie des eaux de Paris. Par M. le comte de Mirabeau
    (1785)

Réponse du comte de Mirabeau à l'écrivain des administrateurs de la Compag-
    nie des eaux de Paris (1785)

Dénonciation au public d'un nouveau projet d'agiotage . . . (1786)

Seconde lettre contre la Compagnie d'assurances pour les incendies à Paris et
    contre l'agiotage en générale (1786)

Tableau raisonné de l'état actuel de la Banque de Saint-Charles (1786)

Dénonciation de l'agiotage au Roi et à l'Assemblée des Notables par le comte
    de Mirabeau (1787)

Suite de la Dénonciation de l'agiotage par le comte de Mirabeau (1788)

Point de banqueroute, ou lettre à un créancier de l'État sur l'impossibilité de la
    banqueroute nationale . . . (1787)

De la foi publique envers les créanciers de l'État (1788)

These works cover a vast stretch of financial and political history, far more than one can discuss in a single essay. But one can examine this literature at a critical turning point, the point where finance turned into politics between July 1785 and February 1787.

The *baissiers* had got along well with Étienne de Calonne, the controller general and a key figure in the government in the early 1780s, because he had favored low discount rates at the Caisse d'escompte and moderate dividends for the Banque d'Espagne, the two companies whose shares were the object of the fiercest speculation. But in 1785 Clavière and the other bears gambled huge sums on a drop in the shares of the Compagnie des eaux de Paris, a company that Calonne was trying to shore up. The controller general had his own reasons for supporting it: He had received 230,000 livres' worth of its shares as a gratification from the king when he assumed the direction of France's finances in 1783. According to a report submitted to the National Assembly in 1790, Calonne had secretly subsidized the company from the national treasury, first with an advance of 1,200,000 livres in 1784, and ultimately with payments that came to 20,000,000 livres in all. It would be too simple, however, to interpret fiscal policy during the last three years of the Old Regime as nothing more than an attempt by the minister to feather his own nest. Calonne was also trying to prevent a general collapse of the stock market—and, indeed, of the entire financial system of the monarchy.[13]

Clavière too had no interest in provoking a crash, but his speculations turned him against Calonne's policy and, at the most crucial moment of the prerevolution, against Calonne himself. By July 1785 the shares of the Compagnie des eaux had soared from 800 to 3600 livres apiece. Clavière had contracted to supply a bull speculator named Mazois with one hundred shares at 1,600 livres in March 1787. To bring the price down, he set Mirabeau's stable of writers to work on a pamphlet, *Sur les actions de la Compagnie des eaux de Paris,* which contained all the usual arguments of the bears. The company was not a bad thing in itself, they conceded, speaking collectively as "Mirabeau." It was established to bring drinking water to Parisians by means of pumps and pipes in place of the old system of dipping tubs in the Seine. But it would never be profitable. The costs of maintaining a steam pump and of laying hundreds of leagues of wooden pipe would never be offset by revenue, and the whole project might be scuttled by a more sensible plan to supply Paris with water by diverting the Yvette River. In fact, the enterprise was nothing more than a pretext for the *haussiers* to make money by inflating the company's assets so that they could boost its shares up to 5,000 livres and then dump them on unsuspecting "fathers of families."[14]

The argument worked well enough to knock 500 livres off the share price within a month. It also provoked a counterattack by the propagandist of the bulls, Beaumarchais, who defended the profitability of the company and derided Mirabeau's "Mirabelles" as a poor attempt to rescue his patrons among the bears. This mockery stung Mirabeau into writing most of the rebuttal to the rebuttal by himself. Far from denying his connection with Clavière, he proclaimed that he glorified in it, for the interests of the *baisse* coincided with those of the public; everyone except *agioteurs* stood to gain by keeping stocks in line with assets. Mirabeau went further. He asserted that the bulls were supported by "men in power." The abuses of the Bourse derived from an evil, insidious source, "stockjobbing in the court."[15]

Such phrases were not bandied about lightly in eighteenth-century pamphlets. The informed public knew that "men in power" referred to the government and that Mirabeau was identifying "stockjobbing" with Calonne. Soon after publishing his outburst in December 1785, Mirabeau departed for safer territory and new fields of intrigue in Berlin, leaving Brissot to defend the interests of Clavière, while Beaumarchais spoke for the bulls and Calonne. Beaumarchais, who had his own portfolio of shares in the Eaux and years of experience in politicofiscal imbroglios, also helped direct the strategy of the Compagnie des eaux in 1786. It consisted of grafting a fire insurance and firefighting company onto the Compagnie des eaux so that the new waterworks would serve several purposes at the same time. By expanding the functions of the company, Beaumarchais hoped to drive up the value of its stock, and therefore Clavière replied with another pamphlet attack on stockjobbing among the bulls.

The new pamphlet, written by Brissot and published anonymously in June 1786, brought the financial polemics one step closer to political insubordination. Its very title, *Dénonciation au public d'un nouveau projet d'agiotage,* anticipated the climactic pamphlet in the series, *Dénonciation de l'agiotage,* which was the most powerful barrage of propaganda in the agitation that drove Calonne from the government in April 1787. In this preliminary *Dénonciation,* Brissot deployed all the standard arguments of the bear group

and stretched them to the breaking point. Paris did not need a commercial fire brigade like that of London, he claimed, because its
houses were made of stone, London's predominantly of wood. Fire
insurance in Paris was a still worse idea, because it would encour-
age people to burn down their houses, despite the stone, in order
to collect indemnities. And the potential damage to public morality represented a far greater danger than the physical devastation.
Beaumarchais's professional firemen, "vile mercenaries," if they
succeeded in putting out fires, would also extinguish *pitié* or com-
passion, which Rousseau had shown to be the fundamental virtue
that held society together. Volunteer firemen, moved by the suffering of their fellow citizens, constantly replenished society's reser-
voir of *pitié*. By eliminating them, the Compagnie des eaux would
destroy civic virtue. But virtue meant nothing to bull speculators:
"They don't care if they corrupt souls and ossify hearts." Their
stockjobbing represented the very opposite of the democratic,
egalitarian spirit described by Rousseau in his account of republican festivals, but amateur firefighting epitomized that spirit: "In this
sacred activity, all social distinctions disappear among the citizens:
magistrates, soldiers, churchmen, artisans, all are merged, all are
linked together." In short, Brissot supported Clavière with the same
kind of Rousseauistic moralizing as he had used against the Genevan
aristocrats in *Le Philadelphien à Genève,* but now he aimed it at Clavière's enemies on the Bourse in order to bring down the price of
shares in the Compagnie des eaux.[16]

Meanwhile Clavière attempted to undercut the company in his
own manner, by promoting the project to supply water to Paris by
diverting the Yvette River and by developing a scheme for a rival
insurance company. The conflict between these speculations came
to a head in July 1786, when the shareholders of the Compagnie
des eaux formally voted to include firefighting and insurance in
their water supply business. Clavière countered this move by arguing

that it nullified his *marché à terme* with Mazois. As he explained in a
letter to his fellow *baissier* Théophile Casenove, the expanded company could be considered a new enterprise, so he had no obligation
to provide Mazois on the agreed date with shares in the old one.
Brissot reproduced this argument in another pamphlet, *Seconde lettre contre La Compagnie d'assurance pour les incendies,* which again
attacked the inflation of shares in language that was designed to
produce a run on them. After a long diatribe against the maneuvers
of the Compagnie des eaux, Brissot blasted the entire range of
haussier speculations and particularly the efforts of a cabal led by a
"stock-jobbing priest" (evidently the abbé d'Espagnac) to force up
the value of shares in the Compagnie des Indes. This theme anticipated the most sensational section of the *Dénonciation de l'agiotage,*
and it linked the operations on the Bourse directly to the government:
"Stockjobbers commonly join forces with powerful men, who
solicit new privileges and new favors from the government in order
to bolster the extravagant prices of shares." Everything was in place
for the final round of financial propaganda, which pitted the bears
against Calonne himself, just as the first Assembly of Notables gathered to consider his desperate proposals to stave off royal bankruptcy by redesigning the kingdom's system of taxation.[17]

The *Dénonciation de l'agiotage* appeared under Mirabeau's name
on March 6, 1787, two weeks after the Notables began their deliberations. Already in January, the clandestine gazetteers noted that
Clavière was leading the *baissiers* in a furious struggle against the abbé
d'Espagnac and others who were gambling on a boom in the shares
of the Compagnie des eaux and the Compagnie des Indes.[18] Clavière's journal of accounts shows that his own gambles committed
him to heavy speculations on futures of the Indes as well as the
Eaux. On September 12, 1786, he recorded a sale *à terme* of 100
shares to Baroud; on September 23, 150 shares to d'Espagnac. An
entry in his cashbox book for March 28, 1787, suggests that he had

paid for the *Dénonciation* itself: "Paid Hardouin [a Parisian printer] for the printing of the memoir against Mazois . . . 204 livres 10 sols." On the previous day, the radical enthusiasts for the American Revolution in the Gallo-American Society noted in their minutes that Clavière had been unable to attend a meeting because he had gone into hiding. They deplored the "persecution" of him, and in a clear allusion to the *Dénonciation de l'agiotage* they voted to support his "patriotic efforts . . . to spread light concerning various questions of high politics and finance." Politics and finance had finally been joined, but the juncture took a curious form: While the Gallo-Americans applauded his patriotism and enlightenment, Clavière was fighting the government from the Bourse.

The point is worth stressing because Mirabeau's biographers, following a somewhat misleading account by Étienne Dumont, have failed to recognize Clavière's crucial role in the production of the *Dénonciation de l'agiotage,* despite the testimony of some well-informed contemporaries.[20] To be sure, Mirabeau contributed a great deal to the success of the pamphlet, if only by putting his name on it. He had returned to Paris in January 1787, and after failing to receive an important enough appointment by Calonne, he had decided to attack the controller general openly in a work that would continue the line of *dénonciations* developed in 1786. But, as in 1786, he mainly supplied the rhetoric. Clavière and some other bear speculators, notably Benjamin Panchaud, provided the substance of the argument, using hack writers like Brissot and Gorsas to compose the text. Brissot alluded to his collaboration only briefly in his memoirs, but Gorsas published a full account of the whole operation in 1792: "In 1786 (a slip for 1787) Mirabeau the elder loaned his name for the famous work entitled De l'agiotage, which some persons have attributed in part to me—and they are not wrong, at least not concerning the draft of some chapters, but as to the financial calculations, they belong to Panchaud and some others: I invoke the testimony of the minister Clavière on that score."

Gorsas went on to explain how he directed the printing, using family connections and clandestine presses in Troyes: "The copy, written and dispatched by Panchaud and others, was addressed to me at the Inn of the Mule c/o the innkeeper, a relative of mine named Coquet. It was at my residence in Versailles, rue des Bour donnois, that the precious pack [of printed copies] was delivered. It was under the very nose of that evil despot Calonne, and despite all his spies, that I had it sent on to Paris."[21]

The bear group had to resort to such hugger-mugger because this time, in attacking the bulls, they directed their fire at the government itself. To be sure, "Mirabeau" adopted the pose of a philosopher who condemned all attempts to make money by manipulating the Bourse instead of by cultivating the earth. But his indignation fell exclusively on the *agioteurs,* who added fictitious value to shares by caballing to force up their price and who were supported in their evil maneuvers by "party leaders among influential men in power, among those exercising authority." Mirabeau linked the government to all the speculations of the bull group for the last two years. Then, in the heart of the pamphlet, he exposed a conspiracy of *haussiers* to inflate the price of shares in the Compagnie des Indes so they could consummate their *à terme* speculations by dumping them on innocent investors. Although "Mirabeau" did not reveal the details of the plot, he printed a "Plan of the abbé d'Espagnac's operations" and charged that the government itself was implicated: "That class of financiers who are honored by the confidence of the Prince, who are in charge of the state's coffers, who oversee the deposit of its income and the payment of its expenses, acquire through their functions a vast amount of credit. They are the ones—yes, it is they—who first demonstrated the possibility of stock jobbing with huge sums of money."[22]

"Mirabeau" did not mention Calonne by name, but the message was clear: The controller general was diverting millions from the treasury to create an artificial bull market while at the same time calling upon the Notables to sanction drastic new taxes on the pretext that the treasury had run dry.

The *baissiers* and their pamphleteers probably did not know how effectively they had scored a hit because they had only caught a glimpse of one of the greatest scandals in the history of French finance. Calonne had secretly advanced *assignations* (notes of credit) from the government to sustain a *hausse* in the shares of the Compagnie des Indes and the Compagnie des eaux by means of *à terme* purchases. But the shares had not risen enough for the *haussiers* to be able to pay back the assignations in March, when they became due at the Ministry of War. The abbé d'Espagnac freed his fellow speculators in the bull group from this predicament by purchasing 32,500 of the Indes shares that they had contracted to buy at a future date. He went on to buy up others as well, until he had concluded *à terme* contracts for 46,000 shares. That was 9,000 more than existed in circulation, so the bulls could not possibly supply the shares they had sold. Therefore d'Espagnac could dictate terms for a settlement, compounding the difficulties of Calonne's position during the critical weeks before the opening of the Assembly of Notables. Although the *baissiers* had not discovered the full extent of the scandal, they had found enough to implicate Calonne in the secret maneuvers of their enemies, the *haussiers*. They made the controller general look like the evil genius behind all the shady dealings on the Bourse, the embodiment of *agiotage*.[23]

This view of Calonne creates a problem because historians have generally given him a good press. Some have gone so far as to hail the reform program he presented to the Assembly of Notables as an eighteenth-century "New Deal." And most would agree that his measures represented a desperate attempt to save the monarchy from bankruptcy at a time when the annual deficit had grown beyond one hundred million livres. The Notables, however, saw Calonne differently. Many of them, including liberals like Lafayette, did not believe a deficit existed. Necker had assured them that the treasury enjoyed a surplus of ten million livres a year in 1781, and a strong current of Neckerite sympathies worked against Calonne from within the Notables. From without, a powerful wave of propaganda made Calonne appear as the central figure in a world of decadent courtiers and despotic ministers. A whole genre of "Calonniana" developed in the pamphlet literature of 1787–1788. Like the "Maupeouana" of 1771–1774, it made the government look rotten by depicting the king's key minister as a moral monster. It struck the same tone of righteous, Rousseauistic indignation that Brissot had maintained through all his pamphlets for Clavière, and it aroused enough outrage among the public to help drive Calonne from the government and ultimately from France.[24]

The Rousseauistic rhetoric compounds the historical problem because today it rings so false. It makes the modern reader inclined to detect a double dose of hypocrisy in the opposition to Calonne, a hypocritical defense of tax privileges on the part of the Notables and a disingenuous defense of stock market speculations by Clavière and the *baissiers*. But historians can be too quick to conclude that they have understood something when they have identified a vested interest lurking behind it. They can become victims of their own superior hindsight. If they fail to take account of what events meant to contemporaries, they can misconstrue the events themselves. We know in retrospect that the caricaturing of Calonne was exaggerated and that it propagated an inaccurate view of French finance. But in its very success it expressed a deeper truth, which was crucial to the outbreak of the French Revolution: The government's version of affairs had ceased to be convincing; the men in power had lost their command of public opinion; the whole regime had begun to appear illegitimate in the eyes of its subjects.

The financial pamphleteering expressed only one of several

ideological currents that fed the general discontent, but it is especially revealing because it shows how the process worked, how
ideas filtered into everyday life and colored the perception of current events. The battles on the Bourse fascinated the public, as one
can see by the extensive coverage of them in clandestine newslet-
ters like the *Mémoires secrets pour servir à l'histoire de la République des
lettres en France*. Bulls and bears in ferocious combat, fortunes made
and lost overnight, public figures dragged into the mud: The stock
market scandals made one of the greatest news stories of the prerevolutionary decade. But there was more to it all than money.
When Clavière subsidized the pamphlets of Brissot, he certainly
meant to defend his speculations, but their collaboration went far
beyond betting on a *baisse*. The Rousseauistic moralizing that runs
through this financial propaganda also appears everywhere in their
activities outside the Bourse, including their agitation for ideals that
they identified with American republicanism. When the Gallo-
American Society voted to support Clavière in his "patriotic" stand
against Calonne, it had two items on its agenda: first, a reading of a
legal tract by Nicolas Bergasse, who had turned a spectacular adultery trial into a denunciation of the entire regime; second, a discussion of a book about America that was then being written by
Brissot and Clavière and that treated morality as the most important factor in Franco-American trade. It may strike us as strange
that the United States, adultery, and commerce should have been
equally urgent topics in the deliberations of a prerevolutionary
société à penser, but then prerevolutionary French radicals did not
think as we do.[25]

Sometime in mid-1789 Clavière tried his hand at a declaration
of the rights of man. His draft included this clause: "The preserva-
tion of morals being absolutely necessary for the maintenance of
the social contract, all financial activities in the public sector must
be considered in relation to morality."[26] There was no speculation *à*

la baisse riding on that statement. Perhaps Clavière really did understand the Bourse according to ideas derived from Rousseau's *Social Contract*. Perhaps the most significant aspect of his pamphleteering with Brissot is not that they meant to make money but that they meant what they said.

THE SKELETONS IN THE
CLOSET: HOW HISTORIANS
PLAY GOD

HARD FACTS HAVE GONE SOFT. There is no denying it, no matter where you took a stand during the last decades while the waves of relativism swept over the intellectual landscape. Biographers may still favor metaphors like digging in the archives, but who believes in quarrying out nuggets of reality? Words like "facts" and "truth" make us uncomfortable and stir the urge to run for protective covering. If you are writing a biography, begin it with disclaimers. An introduction should surround the subject with a warning: We can never know the "real" Virginia Woolf or Teddy Roosevelt, and any reader who suspects the writer of unsophistication should be made to enter the book through a discourse on method.

I was recently writing a protective prolegomenon to a biographical study of Jacques-Pierre Brissot, the leader of the Girondists during the French Revolution. Before I deleted it from my screen's memory, I thought back over the thirty-six years in which I had been tracking this man through the archives. I came upon him first in the Bibliothèque municipale d'Orléans, in 1965. I was the only foreigner who had ever knocked on the library's door, and the man who opened it, the deputy librarian named Le Maire, gave me a cordial welcome. He even offered to show me around the city. Because the tour began with the town hall and because my French

was too feeble to understand much of it, I decided that M. le Maire
must be the mayor of Orléans; and I marveled at the warmth of my
reception. Where else, I thought, would the respect for research
be so great that even a green postgraduate student was given the
red-carpet treatment? Only in France.

Eventually my command of the language proved strong enough
for me to understand that my host was responsible for the library's
archives, and I began to suspect the reason for his hospitality when
he asked me, somewhat tentatively, *"Vous êtes Protestant?"* Although I
am an atheist, my French was not up to a theological confrontation.
I opted for simplicity: *"Oui, Monsieur." "Nous sommes plusieurs,"* he
answered with a smile. Soon he was pointing out underground
shelters where the Huguenots hid from persecution during the
reign of Louis XIV. After that he gave me the key to the library, a
skeleton key that would open everything from the front door to the
closets with medieval manuscripts. I certainly would want to work
after supper, when the library was closed, and during the weekend.
Protestants worked hard. And I could help myself to the documents. Protestants could be trusted.

In the archives after dark I found my first manuscript reference
to Jacques-Pierre Brissot. He too helped Protestants. He wrote in
favor of their emancipation during the 1770s and 1780s, when they
were still denied the right to a civil existence—that is, to marry
and inherit property. He also agitated against the death penalty and
against slavery. He was a passionate Rousseauist, who had actually
witnessed an abortive revolution inspired by Rousseau's ideas in
Geneva in 1782. His idealism fed his enthusiasm for the American
Revolution and all things American, which he celebrated in books
and pamphlets, one more radical than the other. As explained in the
previous chapter, he founded a Gallo-American Society in company
with Étienne Clavière, a Genevan financier and refugee from the
failed revolution of 1782; Hector Saint John de Crèvecoeur, the author

of *Letters from an American Farmer*, which, when transmogrified into Rousseauistic French, had taken Paris by storm; and Nicolas Bergasse, a radical lawyer and notorious Mesmerist. The club did not last long, but it generated enough documentation for me to write a B.Phil. thesis about it at the University of Oxford. I had tried to follow the ideological currents coursing through Jefferson's Paris. And in 1788, when Brissot left Paris for a tour of the United States, I continued to trail him. His path led back to revolutionary France, where he founded *Le Patriote français*, one of the most radical newspapers from the new Left in 1789, and helped found the French Society of the Friends of the Blacks, an influential antislavery society, which also functioned as a political club. For me, the trajectory of Brissot's career led through all the best causes of the eighteenth century and linked the Enlightenment to the Revolution.

It was therefore quite a jolt when I opened a folder in the papers of Jean-Charles-Pierre Lenoir, lieutenant general of police in Paris from August 1774 to May 1775 and from June 1776 to August 1785, in the library of Orléans and found this note in Lenoir's hand: "Brissot remained in Paris [after his release from the Bastille, where he had been imprisoned by *lettre de cachet* from July 12 to September 10, 1784]. He came to offer his services to the police. I refused them, but for about a year he maintained espionage relations with one of the secretaries in that department who presented his reports to me, and he was paid for those reports. Shortly before my retirement, Brissot was still employed as a spy for the police."

Brissot a police spy? A hard fact? Lenoir included that statement among some notes that he intended to assemble into a draft of his memoirs but never completed. He wrote sometime after 1800, when he was living outside France as a refugee from a revolution that he hated. Perhaps he meant to denigrate the Revolution by blackening the name of one of its most eminent leaders. But Lenoir had no personal quarrel with Brissot. None of the other references

in his papers suggests willful mendacity. On the contrary, his contemporaries and biographers generally described him as an honest
and capable civil servant. One might fudge the issue by noting that
"espionage" could involve writing relatively innocent reports about
authors and public opinion. But the Parisians abhorred police spies
well before 1789, when they lynched at least one of them. And Lenoir
used explicit language: Brissot was employed and paid "as a spy for
the police." Thirty-six years later I still find myself disturbed by the
irreducible either/or quality of the question: Either Brissot spied for
police, or he did not. Either Lenoir told the truth, or he was lying.

Orléans was the first stop on a research trip that ended in a truly
great and virtually untapped archive, the papers of Brissot's publisher, the Société typographique de Neuchâtel (STN) in Switzerland. The STN printed large numbers of pirated and prohibited
books, which it smuggled across the Jura Mountains and sold
everywhere in France. Similar publishers and wholesalers had
sprung up all around France's borders, and they did a huge business, thanks to the restrictions imposed on publishing within the
kingdom by censorship, the booksellers' guilds, and the book
police. The papers of the STN—50,000 letters and all sorts of
account books—are the only ones that have survived from this vast
industry. They include 119 unpublished letters of Brissot, as I had
learned by writing to the library of Neuchâtel after coming upon a
footnote in a book of local history.

The letters were waiting for me when I arrived: 119 letters in a
mountain of documents concerning every aspect of the publishing
industry from buying paper to selling books. Unable to resist the
temptation, I began sampling letters by other authors. To my
amazement, I turned up one by a still more famous leader of the
French Revolution, Jean-Paul Marat.

Marat was born in the village of Boudry near Neuchâtel and
completed his schooling in Neuchâtel's *collège* before embarking on

a career as a doctor and scientist in France and England. The letter, addressed to Frédéric-Samuel Ostervald, a family friend and one of the founders of the STN, included a long, cantankerous defense of Marat's most ambitious work, *De l'homme, ou des principes et des lois de l'influence de l'âme sur le corps et du corps sur l'âme* (Amsterdam, 1775–1776), three volumes. It revealed a great deal about Marat's state of mind and early career. But its most important aspect turned out to be its date, May 14, 1776. At that time, according to several of his biographers, Marat was in prison for having stolen one hundred pounds worth of coins and medals from the Ashmolean Museum in Oxford. As the story went, he had been teaching French at Warrington Academy, Lancashire, under an alias, Jean-Pierre Le Maître. He defended himself eloquently at his trial, perhaps by invoking the principle proclaimed in his *Plan de législation criminelle*: "Whoever steals in order to live, when he cannot do otherwise, only makes use of his rights." This Le Maître then escaped from prison in time to reappear in Paris as Marat, whose existence as doctor to the Gardes du corps du comte d'Artois can be documented from June 1777. The story had enough plausibility and more than enough fascination to touch off polemics that stretched back to an article in the *Glasgow Star* of March 4, 1793. But it was wrong. The letter I held in my hand was written from France before the jailbreak in England. It proved that the whole debate turned on a case of mistaken identity.

Without meaning to, I had declared Brissot guilty of spying and Marat innocent of theft. I was pronouncing verdicts about two individuals whom I had never met and who could never defend themselves because they had died in a far-off revolution two hundred years ago. Was this a proper exercise of the historian's vocation?

Back to Brissot. Now that I have published all those letters along with a biographical essay, I realize that I have never stopped living with the man since 1968, when I decided to abandon a full-scale

biography of him. I gave up that project because I considered it
more important to undertake another one, the history of books, a
new kind of subject, which emerged from exposure to the archives
in Neuchâtel. A five-hundred-page draft of a life of Brissot lies in
the bottom of a drawer in my office. Should I try to breathe new
life in it, or have I spent so much of my own life chasing other hares
that I could never catch his scent again? Is he worth the trouble?
Does he really matter?

Most historians probably would come up with two arguments
for the importance of studying Brissot. First, of course, he was one
of the dozen most prominent leaders of the French Revolution;
the more we know about him, the better. He was identified with
the "Brissotin" or Girondist phase of the Revolution, the last period
of moderation before the onset of the Terror. He and his allies were
republicans, idealists, radicals in their way, but not men of blood.
They can be romanticized, as in Lamartine's *Histoire des Girondins*,
but they cannot be dismissed as trivial. Quite the opposite, they
stood for the highest principles, and most of them, Brissot
included, went bravely to the guillotine. In a half dozen biographies
Brissot appears as the epitome of idealism in action. The most
recent of them, by Leonore Loft, compares him with Nelson
Mandela.

Second, Brissot appears in the biographies and general works on
the eighteenth century as the incarnation of a crucial process, the
transition from Enlightenment to Revolution. The connection
between those two phenomena often looks problematic, but Brissot wrote Enlightenment tracts before 1789 and championed
Enlightened causes afterward. Daniel Mornet, the greatest authority on the intellectual origins of the French Revolution, described
him as "the perfect image of all the aspirations of a generation."
Whoever can find the key to Brissot's life may be able to unlock the
most important problems of his times—not to resolve them defin-

itively, of course, but to show how a representative individual lived through them and incorporated them in the basic pattern of his life.

The letters in Neuchâtel certainly open up a new perspective on the life of Brissot because they show how an obscure provincial youth tried to make a name for himself as a writer. Brissot had no protectors or connections of any importance, so he had to write his way into the Republic of Letters. His father, a fairly well-off caterer (*maître cuisinier et traiteur*) in Chartres, wanted him to be a lawyer. But while completing his secondary education, Jacques-Pierre fell under the spell of Voltaire, and while clerking for attorneys, first in Chartres, then in Paris, he took to writing essays on subjects like the absurdities in the epistles of Saint Paul and the iniquities in France's system of criminal law. His father, a devout Catholic, threatened to disinherit him and finally left him only 4,000 livres, a minimal "légitime," from a fortune of more then 100,000 livres, when he died in 1779. Jacques-Pierre used some of the money, 600 livres, to buy a perfunctory law degree from the University of Reims but soon abandoned the law for literature. He explained in his *Mémoires*: "Henceforth free, I resolved to devote myself entirely to the profession of writing."

Was writing a profession at that time? This question occupies a central place in the sociology of literature as developed by Robert Escarpit, Pierre Bourdieu, and Alain Viala. Brissot's memoirs reveal something of the strategy he pursued in order to get ahead in his career. He appealed for help to Voltaire and d'Alembert, competed in prize essay contests after the example of Rousseau, cultivated contacts in literary circles, and wrote one philosophical treatise after another. Although he failed to break into the front ranks of the *philosophes*, he attracted enough attention to be persecuted by the state. He escaped from the first *lettre de cachet* issued for his arrest in 1779, but the second led to his imprisonment in the Bastille for two months in 1784. A Bastille record on top of a bibliography of

Enlightenment tracts provided him with a perfect pedigree in 1789, when he emerged as a prototypical *philosophe* turned revolutionary.

Brissot cast himself in this role when he described his prerevolutionary career in his memoirs, and his biographers have followed suit. I did too when I started reading his dossier in the papers of the STN in 1965. In some ways the new material confirmed the old picture from the memoirs. It showed how Brissot published most of his books. Too obscure and too outspoken to sell his copy to publishers in France, he paid the Swiss to print it and hoped to cover his costs by marketing the editions through middlemen in France's vast underground book trade. His most ambitious book, *Théorie des lois criminelles* (1780), certainly deserves a place among the legal treatises of the Enlightenment, although it is derived almost entirely from the more original work of Cesare Beccaria. It impressed the STN's principal director, Frédéric-Samuel Ostervald, who took a somewhat fatherly interest in Brissot. The two met when Ostervald made a business trip to Paris in 1780, and they seemed to hit it off. By 1781 Brissot's letters to Ostervald had taken on a confidential tone, and his confidences concerned his efforts to win fame and fortune as a writer.

Of course the best of writers may confess at times to extravagant ambition and describe their careers as moves in a game of getting ahead. But I was surprised to find the theme of self-advancement so pervasive in Brissot's letters. They show him seeking introductions, cultivating endorsements, trying to get his name in journals, soliciting favorable reviews, demanding special treatment in essay contests, and maneuvering to get elected to academies. In his memoirs he claimed that he scorned academies because of their exclusiveness, but in his letters he asks Ostervald to promote him in the STN's *Journal helvétique* as "M. Brissot de Warville, lawyer at the Parlement of Paris, member of diverse academies, already known by his *Théorie des lois criminelles* of which we have spoken in our earlier issues and by a memoir on the same subject crowned last year at the Académie de Châlons." He also claimed in his memoirs that he had always hated kings, but he directed Ostervald to send specially bound copies of his books to Frederick II and Catherine II: "I am making my debut in literature, and my name is not at all known. . . . As I want this to work to cause a sensation, it must have the most publicity possible, it must be sent out everywhere, to all the crowned heads, and I will spare nothing to that end." After sketching a plan for a treatise on "universal pyrrhonism," Brissot begged d'Alembert to write him a letter that would serve as a preface to it. But when d'Alembert sent only two tepid lines, he abandoned the plan. His connections with the *Courrier de l'Europe*, where he had worked for a while as a proofreader, provided him with some publicity; but he raged at his inability to crack the *Journal de Paris*. He got himself elected to the Académie de Châlons-sur-Marne, but he found it impossible in Paris to advance beyond the Musée of Pilâtre de Rozier, a nonexclusive literary club where anyone could read a paper on anything. Endless lobbying with the Société économique de Berne got him nowhere in its prize essay competition, and none of his books produced the slightest splash, despite his attempts to orchestrate favorable reviews.

Brissot's endless stream of proposals to the publisher also suggests self-promotion and entrepreneurship rather than dedication to Enlightenment. He seemed ready to write on almost anything: a ten-volume digest of the proceedings of the Académie des inscriptions et belles-lettres, a ten-volume biographical dictionary of men of letters, a compilation of works on education, a treatise on how to learn languages, a history of criminal law. All these works sounded like potboilers, and none of them ever made it into print, because Brissot wanted to sell them to the STN. In proposing the anthology of writings from the Académie des inscriptions et belles-lettres, he explained that he would churn out copy by recruiting hacks: "I will direct a group of subaltern laborers." Brissot actually speculated on two compilations of his own, a ten-volume *Biblio-thèque philosophique du législateur* and a *Correspondance universelle sur ce qui intéresse le bonheur de l'homme et de la société*, which was supposed to go on indefinitely but stalled after volume 2. Their titles suggest high-mindedness, but their contents show them to be nothing more than scissors-and-paste jobs. In fact Brissot never wrote anything of any distinction—at least not as far as I could tell after plowing through thousands of pages of his prose. His most important work, *Théorie des lois criminelles*, was, as mentioned, little more than a pastiche of Beccaria's *Dei delitti e delle pene*, and his most pretentious publication, *De la vérité, ou méditations sur les moyens de parvenir à la vérité dans toutes les connaissances humaines* (1782), merely rehashed the standard commonplaces of Enlightenment thought.

The only works by Brissot that attracted any attention from his contemporaries were pamphlets; and insofar as they made him known at all, they gave him a reputation as a vehement polemicist. After reading his *Le Philadelphien à Genève* (1783), Jacques Mallet du Pan described him as an example of the most vulgar element in literature: "Men of letters these days are becoming riffraff [*canaille*], and the vilest kind of riffraff, because they combine impudence with cowardice." And Jean-François de La Harpe dismissed him as a boorish, fifth rate follower of Rousseau. But others seemed to take his measure more accurately. When Friedrich von Freudenreich informed Ostervald that the Société économique de Berne would not bend its rules, as Brissot had requested, in order to give him an inside track in a prize essay competition, he observed: "At his age [then twenty-eight], to put himself forward as a totally competent judge of all aspects of philosophy, politics, and law, to present himself as a new Archimedes . . . is to exhibit a degree of self-importance of which only a young French man of letters is capable."

That assessment struck me as close to the mark. Insofar as he could be considered a *philosophe*, Brissot represented the High

Enlightenment at middle brow. But why consider him as a philosopher at all? Because he presented himself that way in his memoirs and because his biographers modeled their interpretations on his. He appears in a different light, however, when seen through his correspondence with the STN. In addition to proposing potboilers that never got published, he published pamphlets that never were attributed to him because they were anonymous. The STN printed four of them, all unknown to his previous biographers. One was an amateurish essay about studying languages, one a polemical account of the literary scene in Paris, and two were tendentious broadsides about international relations. When I read the latter, I thought I recognized the Brissot of 1792. Instead of discussing issues seriously, they heaped abuse on France's enemies and struck a vituperative tone, which sounded something like his speeches to the Jacobin Club a decade later, when he did more than anyone else to embroil the Revolution in a disastrous war. The corpus of Brissot's works, when reconstructed through the archives of his publisher, does not appear very philosophical, and Brissot himself does not look much like a philosopher.

Perhaps, however, I have been infected by the bias of Brissot's enemies. I must admit that once I began to read his works against the grain, they lost their luster; and after I pieced together the story behind their publication, they smelled bad. A biographer should beware when he starts to dislike his subject. But once I started, I could not stop. Every bit of evidence that I turned up reinforced my tendency to suspect the man projected in the memoirs, especially when I investigated the financial side of his ventures into literature.

Brissot's inheritance sufficed to pay for the printing of his first books. But when it gave out, he adopted a strategy of pyramiding: the sales of one book were to pay for producing another. It was possible to postpone the reckoning from one publication to the next because of the delays built into the system of payment. Like most authors who commissioned books with the STN, Brissot promised to cover their cost with bills of exchange that matured six months after he received the printed copies. If he could market them fast enough, he could square his accounts. He wrote the bills on his Parisian bookseller, E.-M.-P. Desauges, a wily veteran of the underground, who collaborated with equally shady characters, such as Jacques Revol, a smuggler in Lyons, and the Widow La Noue, a shipping agent with secret stockrooms scattered throughout Versailles. The middlemen had enough expertise to handle their roles effectively; but, as Brissot described them in his letters, they operated on the principle of honor among thieves, and they had no honor. In the end, after all sorts of complications and maneuvers, Desauges refused to accept Brissot's bills of exchange, and Brissot protested that he had been fleeced by a pack of rogues.

He also had another excuse for failing to pay his bills: the police had confiscated a shipment of five hundred copies of his *Théorie des lois criminelles*. Therefore, in his version of his difficulties, he was an innocent who had fallen victim to enemies on both sides in the battles of the books—the agents of royal despotism, on the one hand, and their adversaries from the literary underground, on the other. In fact, however, the situation was more complicated. The underground actually performed its tasks quite well. The shipment made it to widow La Noue's warehouse without a hitch, but Brissot thought he could get it past the inspectors in Paris by having it shipped directly to the headquarters of Lenoir, the lieutenant general of police. Why did he take such an audacious step? He was confident, he explained to the STN, that the police had given him "a secret permission for passage into Paris." But instead of turning the books over to Desauges, Lenoir sent them to Le Camus de Néville, the inspector of the book trade, who promptly confiscated them.

After months of negotiation Néville finally permitted Desauges to sell one hundred copies under the counter and agreed to ship the other four hundred back to the STN, which eventually sent them back again to Desauges by a still safer route. By then they had accumulated so much in shipping charges that Desauges reaffirmed his refusal to pay the bill of exchange. Meanwhile, thanks to more favoritism from the police, Brissot had got clearance to ship his *Bibliothèque philosophique* into Paris. Although he made only elliptical references to his police contacts in his letters to Neuchâtel, they probably included Lenoir's secretary in charge of the illegal book trade and the Bastille, a M. Martin. In explaining his assurance that the police would tolerate his books, Brissot emphasized, "M. Martin, who seems to hold me in esteem and to be attached to me, assured me of his zeal." The first shipments made it safely, as promised, to Desauges's shop behind the Palais de Justice. But then Brissot overplayed his hand. He printed the prospectus for his *Correspondance universelle* in volume 5 of the *Bibliothèque philosophique* without getting permission from the police. To circulate an illegal prospectus was a serious offense, so the police confiscated the shipment of volume 5, making it impossible to sell the entire, ten-volume set and throwing Brissot's finances into disarray. I concluded that Brissot had indeed suffered from the repressive apparatus of the Old Regime—not, however, because he defied the police, but because he botched his arrangements to collaborate with them.

The full extent of Brissot's indebtedness is a complicated story, which involves his attempt to create a lycée, or literary club, in London, which he modeled on the Musée of Pilâtre de Rozier in Paris. It went broke, he went bankrupt, and after a brief stay in debtor's prison just after his wife gave birth to their first child, he returned to Paris in order to find a financial backer. His main hope was the friend he had made during the troubles in Geneva, Étienne Clavière. But on July 12, 1784, after he had spent an evening discussing his crisis with Clavière, the police carried him off to the Bastille. I calculate his indebtedness at that point as 25,636 livres, the equivalent of eighty years of wages for an ordinary artisan.

Why did the police imprison Brissot? Not, as he said in his memoirs, because of his radical philosophizing, but, as the Bastille records put it, *"pour libelles"*—that is, for slander. In fact his first brush with the police, when he had narrowly escaped the Bastille, had also been for slander, because he had made some nasty remarks about the sex life of a salon lady in a pamphlet called *Le Pot Pourri*. His offense in 1784 was far more serious because the pamphlets attributed to him concerned the sex life of the queen. Brissot had spent much of 1783 and 1784 in a colony of French expatriates in London, who supported themselves by libeling and blackmailing the leading figures of the French court. They were a rum lot— defrocked priests, déclassé noblemen, and down-and-out hack writers—and one of their most cynical slanderers was a marquis turned adventurer named Anne-Gédéon Lafitte de Pelleport. In his memoirs Brissot claimed that he hardly knew Pelleport and did not meet him until 1783. But the first of his letters in the STN archives, dated August 31, 1779, is addressed to Pelleport, who was then in Neuchâtel; and by eighteenth-century standards it is extremely intimate in tone: *"Addio il mio caro. Je vous embrasse. . . ."*

Having lured Pelleport back to France, the police arrested him on the day before they captured Brissot. It seems likely that he implicated Brissot and that Brissot returned the favor during his own interrogations. According to his memoirs and other writings, the police tortured him by shutting him up in an underground cell and cutting him off from all contact with the outside world, including his wife. According to the archives of the Bastille, Brissot was treated well, allowed to walk in the Bastille garden, and saw his wife for the first of several visits on "the 24th [of August], from 9:30 to 10:30."

Did Brissot collaborate on smutty pamphlets like *Les Amours de Charlot et Toinette*, *Le Passe-temps d'Antoinette et du vizir de Vergennes*, *La Naissance du dauphin dévoilée*, and *Le Diable dans un bénitier*? Having read through the elaborate reports by French agents in London that

are scattered through the archives at the Quai d'Orsay, I think it
unlikely. None of the spies linked a specific libel to Brissot, and the
police released him after only two months, whereas they kept
Pelleport behind bars for four years. But as two of his friends
hinted in letters to the STN, Brissot might have helped distribute
some of the pamphlets. And after finding himself betrayed, he may
have told the police everything he knew about Pelleport and the
other London *libellistes*. We cannot verify those hypotheses, however, because Brissot's dossier has disappeared from the archives of
the Bastille. It was given to him after July 14, 1789, by his friend
Pierre Manuel and never seen again.

The ambiguities surrounding Brissot's *embastillement* bear on the
question that has been gnawing at me all these years: was Brissot a
police spy? He mentioned confidential contacts with the police several times in letters to the STN before his imprisonment, and in a
letter written afterward, on February 19, 1785, the STN's agent in
Paris, J.-F. Bornand, reported that Brissot had been meeting with
"M. Martin, first secretary of the lieutenant general of police," and
that Martin had provided him with some inside information about
police measures against book smuggling. Martin could have been
the secretary mentioned in Lenoir's statement about Brissot's spying. And Lenoir's account fits the picture of growing desperation that
emerges from Brissot's correspondence with the STN. It also fits the
way Brissot was pictured at that time by Marat: "There he was [after
his release from the Bastille] in the street, without any resources, and
to add to his misery, burdened with a wife and a baby. It is now notorious that, not knowing what to do, he decided to offer his services
to Lenoir, the lieutenant of police, who made him a royal observor
for 50 écus [150 livres] a month."

Although Marat and Brissot became mortal enemies after 1790,
they were close friends in the 1780s. Marat's account of Brissot's
spying also correlates closely with that of Lenoir. It too, however,

should be read with skepticism because it appeared in Marat's *Ami du peuple* on June 4, 1792 at a moment when he was capable of saying anything. The same accusation, with plenty of inconsistencies and inaccuracies, can be found in a dozen attacks on Brissot by his enemies during the nastiest episodes of political dogfighting from the beginning of the Revolution right up to his trial before the Revolutionary Tribunal, when it led the items on his indictment. Considering the viciousness of the polemics and the tragedy of the outcome, one can only conclude that the case against him remains unproved.

I admit, however, that I believe Brissot probably was a spy. This conviction grew as I read through his letters in Neuchâtel. By 1784 the theme of frustrated ambition had turned into financial desperation, and in the first letter that he wrote to the STN after his release from the Bastille, he confessed that he was ruined. A salary of 150 livres a month from the police could have supported his family, but a lifetime of labor would not have paid off the debts he owed in London and in Neuchâtel. Ultimately he was rescued by Étienne Clavière, who not only gave him loans but also persuaded the STN to take back Brissot's books in lieu of payment for their printing.

The full story of Brissot's attempts to crawl out of bankruptcy between 1784 and 1789 involves a great deal of arithmetic. In order to make sense of it, I found myself working over Clavière's account books in the Archives nationales in Paris. As explained in chapter 7, they had been confiscated by the revolutionary police after the Convention decreed the arrest of Clavière along with the other Girondists, and they showed an impressive series of payments to Brissot during the second half of the 1780s, when Brissot wrote a series of pamphlets designed to promote Clavière's speculations on the Bourse.

Brissot's pamphleteering took him directly into the struggles that brought down the Old Regime, but when the rickety edifice began to fall, he was in America—in order to investigate republicanism first hand, according to his memoirs. Back in America myself, I picked up Brissot's trail in the American Antiquarian Society, the Massachusetts Historical Society, and the New-York Historical Society. Those archives showed that he had been using Clavière's money to speculate on the paper currency of the colonies, which could be worth a fortune if redeemed at anything near their face value by the new federal government. There was nothing illegal about these transactions, although they involved some dubious characters like William Duer and Christopher Gore. There was also no reason to doubt the authenticity of Brissot's enthusiasm for all things American, money included. Brissot even considered emigrating, but word of the coming revolution drew him back to France. He founded *Le Patriote français* three months before the Bastille fell, and his fortune rose with the success of his newspaper. For a few moments in the spring of 1792 he probably was the most powerful man in France. He used his power to have Clavière appointed minister of finances. The Revolution was their greatest speculation, and they went down together in the spring of 1793.

Put that baldly, Brissot's biography looks like a string of lies, the very opposite of the narrative line developed in his memoirs and adopted by all his biographers, except me. Propelled by the sensation of belonging to a minority of one and by the eternal temptation of revisionism, I enlisted in a faculty seminar on psychobiography that was being taught at Harvard in 1967 by Erik Erikson. I gave a paper on Brissot and began by announcing, with some exaggeration, that I could find a lie on every page in Brissot's memoirs. Erikson interrupted. "In psychoanalysis," he said, "we do not speak of lies; we speak of screen memory."

I reworked the paper, purged of references to the Oedipal complex and the stages of infant sexuality, and it was published in the following year: "The Grub Street Style of Revolution: J.-P. Brissot, Police Spy." Rereading it today, I see a lot of anger in it, a lot of 1968 and even of my own biography. I now feel less hostility to Erikson, surrounded as he was by an unfortunate cult of personality, and I feel more sympathy for the notion of screen memory.

How much screening have I been guilty of? I use the word "guilt" because I cannot help asking what Brissot, poor bastard, ever did to me? Something happened after that first encounter with the manuscripts of Lenoir. The facts seemed hard enough, but I kept arranging them in darker patterns. From literary ambition to hack writing, indebtedness, bankruptcy, spying, speculating, jobbing his protector into power, and pushing France into disasters abroad and at home, Brissot turned into the antithesis of the man I had once admired. Can biography get caught in gestalt switching?

The facts have not dissolved into discourse, but they now look different. I now think that Brissot really was an idealist, a true believer in Enlightenment, and when he lied, he believed in his lies. They were authentic, like the tricks of memory in the *Confessions* of Rousseau. Brissot wrote his memoirs in prison, in the shadow of the guillotine, after reading the *Confessions* for the sixth time. The memoirs lack the ring of genius, but they do not ring false. They are the authentic memoirs of a Grub Street hack caught up in a revolution that was partly of his own making. God rest his soul. God have mercy on all of us.

You may suspect me of losing my grip on facts and of slipping into postmodernism or even the sort of superstition that the Enlightenment combatted. So let me cite a final fact, which I dug out of the same archives in Neuchâtel: the death of Jean-Élie Bertrand on February 24, 1779.

Bertrand was a Protestant pastor turned man of letters. After marrying Ostervald's daughter, he became one of the three directors of the STN. To judge from his letters and those of his friends as well as two volumes of his sermons, he was a sympathetic character: a good husband and father, generous, cultivated, open-minded, and committed to the moderate, Swiss variety of Enlightenment. He died at age forty, leaving a widow and three children. That loss forever marked their lives, as you can see by following its effects through letters from the family. Other letters, mostly about business, also lead to Bertrand's dossier. They kept carrying me back to it when I was tracing other stories through other dossiers. And every time I opened the dossier of Bertrand, I knew what would happen.

At one point he assures a correspondent that his cough is getting better. At another, he cannot make a meeting because he is bedridden. Then things brighten up; he has been back in the printing shop. But the awful, inevitable day is only a few letters away: February 24, Bertrand is gone forever.

I can replay the dying of Bertrand in many ways, stop it at any point, run it backward or fast forward it into links with other dossiers that relate to his in endless combinations.

What am I doing? What every historian does: playing God.

As Saint Augustine explained, God exists outside time. He can replay history as He pleases, backward or forward or all at once.

The historian certainly creates life. He breathes life into the mud that he digs out of the archives. He also passes judgment on the dead. He can't do otherwise: Either Brissot spied for the police or he did not. The facts will not go away, but their pattern changes as I rearrange them, not merely by whatever artistry I can summon up but by gestalt switches: Revolutionary or police spy? Philosopher or literary hack? Rabbit or duck?

Perhaps, however, the either/or approach to biography is flawed. Perhaps life is a bundle of contradictions, and the attempt to impose consistency on it is wrong. Was Brissot both a dedicated revolutionary and a crass spy for the police?

God only knows. The historian knows, but imperfectly, through documents darkly, with help from hubris, by playing God.

NOTES

INTRODUCTION

1. Malvin E. Ring, *Dentistry: An Illustrated History* (New York, 1985), p. 193, and James Wynbrandt, *The Excruciating History of Dentistry* (New York, 1998), pp. 158–62.

2. Jefferson to Madison, September 6, 1789, in Julian P. Boyd, ed., *The Papers of Thomas Jefferson* (Princeton, 1958), p. 396. On the philosophy behind this idea, one of Jefferson's wildest, see Adrienne Koch, *Jefferson and Madison: The Great Collaboration* (New York, 1950), vol. 15, pp. 62–96.

3. Ranke's famous formula is actually more powerful than it appears to be in the phrase commonly quoted in translation. In the original, a preface to his *Histories of the Latin and Germanic Nations from 1494 to 1514,* he wrote that his endeavor was not to judge the past or to instruct the present but ". . . only to show what actually happened": ". . . *Er will bloss zeigen, wie es eigentlich gewesen.*" It is the "only" that carries such heavy weight. Leopold von Ranke, "Vorrede der ersten Ausgabe," *Geschichten der romanischen und germanischen Völker von 1494 bis 1514* in *Leopold von Ranke's Sämmtliche Werke* (Leipzig, 1877), vol. 33, p. vii.

4. See, for example, James Clifford and George E. Marcus, *Writing Culture: The Poetics and Politics of Ethnography* (Berkeley, 1986) and Johannes Fabian, *Time and the Work of Anthropology: Critical Essays, 1971–1991* (Philadelphia, 1991).

5. Louis-Sébastien Mercier, *Tableau de Paris,* ed. Jean-Claude Bonnet (Paris, 1994), vol. 1, chap. 50, pp. 138–39. See also the superb essay by Colin Jones, "Pulling Teeth in Eighteenth-Century Paris," *Past & Present,* no. 166 (February 2000), pp. 100–45.

Chapter 1 THE CASE FOR THE ENLIGHTENMENT

1. John Gray, *Enlightenment's Wake: Politics and Culture at the Close of the Modern Agen* (London: Routledge, 1995), p. 146.

Chapter 2 THE NEWS IN PARIS

1. People have complained about a surfeit of information during many periods of history. An almanac of 1772 referred casually to *"notre siècle de publicité à outrance,"* as if the observation were self-evident: Roze de Chantoiseau, *Tablettes royales de renommée ou Almanach général d'indication,* rpt. in "Les cafés de Paris en 1772" (anonymous), *Extrait de la Revue de poche du 15 juillet 1867* (Paris, n.d.), p. 2. For a typical remark that illustrates the current sense of entering an unprecedented era dominated by information technology, see the pronouncement of David Puttnam quoted in the *Wall Street Journal,* December 18, 1998, p. W3: "We are on the threshold of what has come to be called the Information Society." I should explain that this essay was written for delivery as a lecture and that I have tried to maintain the tone of the original by adopting a relatively informal style in the printed version. More related material is available in an electronic edition, the first article published in the new online edition of the *American Historical Review,* on the World Wide Web, at www.indiana.edu/~ahr, and later at www.history cooperative.org/ahr.

2. I have attempted to develop this argument in an essay on my own experience as a reporter: "Journalism: All the News that Fits We Print," in Robert Darnton, *The Kiss of Lamourette: Reflections in Cultural History* (New York, 1990), chap. 5. See also Michael Schudson, *Discovering the News: A Social History of American Newspapers* (New York, 1978) and Helen MacGill Hughes, *News and the Human Interest Story* (Chicago, 1940).

3. Brian Cowan, "The Social Life of Coffee: Commercial Culture and Metropolitan Society in Early Modern England, 1600–1720" (Ph.D. dissertation, Princeton University, 2000); Qin Shao, "Tempest over Teapots: The Vilification of Teahouse Culture in Early Republican China," *Journal of Asian Studies,* vol. 57 (November 1998), pp. 1009–41; Lawrence Rosen, *Bargaining for Reality: The Construction of Social Relations in a Muslim Community* (Chicago, 1984); Laurie Nussdorfer, *Civic Politics in the Rome of Urban VIII* (Princeton, 1992); João José Reis, *Slave Rebellion in Brazil: The Muslim Uprising of 1835 in Bahia,* trans. Arthur Brakel (Baltimore, 1993); Christopher A. Bayly, *Empire and Information: Intelligence Gathering and Social Communication in India, 1780–1870* (New York, 1996); and Keith Hopkins, *Death and Renewal* (Cambridge, 1983).

4. Planted at the beginning of the century and cut down during the remodeling of the garden in 1781, the Tree of Cracow was such a well-known institution that it was celebrated in a comic opera by Charles-François Panard, *L'Arbre de Cracovie,* performed at the Foire Saint-Germain in 1742. The print reproduced above probably alludes to a theme in that vaudeville production: The tree went "crack" every time someone beneath its branches told a lie. On this and other contemporary sources, see François Rosset, *L'Arbre de Cracovie: Le mythe polonais dans la littérature française* (Paris, 1996), pp. 7–11. The best general account of *nouvellistes* is still in Frantz Funck-Brentano, *Les Nouvellistes* (Paris, 1905), and *Figaro et ses devanciers* (Paris, 1909). As an example of how remarks made beneath the Tree of Cracow spread throughout Paris and Versailles, see

E. J. B. Rathery, ed., *Journal et mémoires du marquis d'Argenson* (Paris, 1862), vol. 5, p. 450.

5. Pierre Manuel, *La Police de Paris dévoilée* (Paris, "L'An second de la liberté" [1790]), vol. 1, p. 206. I have not been able to find the original of this spy report by the notorious Charles de Fieux, chevalier de Mouhy, in Mouhy's dossier in the archives of the Bastille: Bibliothèque de l'Arsenal (hereafter, BA), Paris, ms. 10029.

6. This description relies on the work of Funck-Brentano, *Les Nouvellistes,* and *Figaro et ses devanciers,* but more recent work has modified the picture of the "parish" and its connection to the *Mémoires secrets.* See Jeremy D. Popkin and Bernadette Fort, eds., *The "Mémoires secrets" and the Culture of Publicity in Eighteenth-Century France* (Oxford, 1998); François Moureau, *Répertoire des nouvelles à la main: Dictionnaire de la presse manuscrite clandestine XVIe–XVIIIe siècle* (Oxford, 1999); and Moureau, *De bonne main: La Communication manuscrite au XVIIIe siècle* (Paris, 1993). After studying the voluminous text of the *nouvelles à la main* produced by the "parish" between 1745 and 1752, I have concluded that the copy in the Bibliothèque Nationale de France (hereafter, BNF) contains little information that could not have passed through the censorship administered by the police: BNF, ms. fr. 13701–12. The published version of the *Mémoires secrets,* which covered the period 1762–1787 and first appeared in 1777, is completely different in tone. It was highly illegal and sold widely; see Robert Darnton, *The Corpus of Clandestine Literature in France 1769–1789* (New York, 1995), pp. 119–20.

7. In the case of France, a vast number of excellent books and articles have been published by Jean Sgard, Pierre Rétat, Gilles Feyel, François Moureau, Jack Censer, and Jeremy Popkin. For an overview of the entire subject, see Claude Bellanger, Jacques Godechot, Pierre Guiral, and Fernand Terrou, *Histoire générale de la presse française* (Paris, 1969) and the collective works edited by Jean Sgard, *Dictionnaire des journaux, 1600–1789* (Oxford, 1991), 2 vols., and *Dictionnaire des journalistes, 1600–1789* (1976; rpt. ed., Oxford, 1999), 2 vols.

8. Michael Stolleis, *Staat und Staatsräson in der frühen Neuzeit* (Frankfurt, 1990) and Jochen Schlobach, "Secrètes correspondances: La fonction du secret dans les correspondances littéraires," in Moureau, *De bonne main.*

9. Manuel, *La Police de Paris dévoilée,* vol. 1, pp. 201–02.

10. A. de Boislisle, ed., *Lettres de M. de Marville, Lieutenant-Général de Police, au ministre Maurepas (1742–1747)* (Paris, 1896), vol. 2, p. 262.

11. On literacy, see François Furet and Jacques Ozouf, *Lire et écrire: L'Alphabétisation des Français de Calvin à Jules Ferry* (Paris, 1977), 2 vols.; on public opinion, Keith M. Baker, "Public Opinion as Political Invention," in Baker, *Inventing the French Revolution: Essays on French Political Culture in the Eighteenth Century* (Cambridge, 1990); and Mona Ozouf, "L'Opinion publique," in Keith Baker, ed., *The Political Culture of the Old Regime,* vol. 1, *The French Revolution and the Creation of Modern Political Culture* (Oxford, 1987).

12. [Mathieu-François Pidansat de Mairobert], *Anecdotes sur Mme. la comtesse du Barry* (London, 1775), p. 215.

13. This and the following remarks about Mairobert are based on his dossier in the archives of the Bastille: BA, ms. 11683, and on his dossier in the papers of Joseph d'Hémery, inspector of the book trade: BNF, ms. acq. fr. 10783. See also the article on him in the *Dictionnaire des journalistes*, vol. 2, pp. 787–89.

14. "Observations de d'Hémery du 16 juin 1749," BA, ms. 11683, fol. 52.

15. *Le Portefeuille d'un talon rouge contenant des anecdotes galantes et secrètes de la cour de France*, rpt. as *Le coffret du bibliophile* (Paris, n.d.), 22.

16. BA, ms. 10170. This source, the densest I have been able to find, covers the years 1726–1729. For help in locating the cafés and in mapping them, I would like to thank Sean Quinlan, editorial assistant at the *American Historical Review*, and Jian Liu, reference librarian and collection manager for linguistics, Indiana University Libraries, who worked with the staff of the *AHR* in preparing the electronic version of this essay. The detailed mapping, with excerpts from reports on conversations in eighteen of the cafés, can be consulted in the link entitled "Mapping Café Talk," at www. historycooperative.org/ahr.

17. BA, ms. 10170, fol. 175. For reasons of clarity, I have added quotation marks. The original had none, although it was clearly written in dialogue, as can be seen from the texts reproduced in the electronic version of this essay, at the link titled "Spy Reports on Conversations in Cafés," www.historycooperative.org/ahr.

18. BA, ms. 10170, fol. 176.

19. BA, ms. 10170, fol. 93.

20. BNF, ms. nouv. acq. fr. 1891, fol. 419.

21. Marc Bloch, *Rois thaumaturges: Étude sur le caractère surnaturel attribué à la puissance royale* (Paris, 1924). On contemporary indignation about the route around Paris, see BNF, ms. fr. 13710, fol. 66. For a sober account of Louis XV's relations with the Nesle sisters (there were actually five of them, but contemporary *libelles* usually mentioned only three or sometimes four), see Michel Antoine, *Louis XV* (Paris, 1989), pp. 484–92. My interpretation of political and diplomatic history in these years owes a good deal to Antoine's definitive study.

22. BA, ms. 10029, fol. 129. The incest theme appears in some of the most violent poems and songs attacking Louis XV from 1748 to 1751. One in the Bibliothèque Historique de la Ville de Paris, ms. 649, p. 50, begins, "*Incestueux tyran, traître inhumain, faussaire . . .*"

23. These issues have been dramatized most recently in the controversy aroused by the duplicitous mixture of fact and fiction in Edmund Morris, *Dutch: A Memoir of Ronald Reagan* (New York, 1999); see Kate Masur, "Edmund Morris's *Dutch:* Reconstructing Reagan or Deconstructing History?" *Perspectives*, vol. 37 (December 1999), pp. 3–5. For my part, I would not deny the literary quality of history writing, but I think the invention of anything that is passed off as factual violates an implicit contract between the historian and the reader: whether or not we are certified as professionals by the award of a Ph.D., we historians should never fabricate evidence.

24. Four editions of *Les Amours de Zeokinizul, roi des Kofirans: Ouvrage traduit de l'Arabe du*

voyageur Krinelbol (Amsterdam, 1747, 1747, 1748, and 1770) can be consulted in the BNF, Lb38.554.A-D. All but the first have elaborate keys, usually inserted into the binding from a separate copy, sometimes with manuscript notes. Some notes also appear in the margins of this and the other three works, which also have keys.

25. The following quotations come from BNF, ms. nouv. acq. fr. 1891, fols. 421, 431, 433, 437.

26. BNF, ms. nouv. acq. fr. 10783.

27. BA, ms. 11582, fols. 55–57. See also Mlle. Bonafons's remarks in her second interrogation, fols. 79–80: "*A elle représenté qu'il y a dans cet ouvrage des faits particuliers dont son état ne lui permettait pas naturellement d'avoir connaissance. Interpellée de nous déclarer par qui elle en a été instruite. A dit qu'il ne lui a été fourni aucuns mémoires ni donné aucuns conseils, et que c'est les bruits publics et le hazard qui l'ont déterminée à insérer dans l'ouvrage ce qui s'y trouve.*"

28. Louis-Sébastien Mercier, *Tableau de Paris,* new ed. (Neuchâtel, 1788), vol. 1, p. 282. Mercier also remarked (vol. 6, p. 40); "*Ainsi à Paris tout est matière à chanson; et quiconque, maréchal de France ou pendu, n'a pas été chansonné a beau faire il demeurera inconnu au peuple.*" Among the many historical studies of French songs, see especially Emile Raunié, *Chansonnier historique du XVIIIᵉ siècle* (Paris, 1879–84), 10 vols.; Patrice Coirault, *Formation de nos chansons folkloriques* (Paris, 1953), 4 vols.; Rolf Reichardt and Herbert Schneider, "Chanson et musique populaire devant l'histoire à la fin de l'Ancien Régime," *Dix-huitième siècle,* vol. 18 (1986), pp. 117–44; and Giles Barber, "'Malbrouck s'en va-t-en guerre' or, How History Reaches the Nursery," in Gillian Avery and Julia Briggs, eds., *Children and Their Books: A Collection of Essays to Celebrate the Work of Iona and Peter Opie* (Oxford, 1989), pp. 135–63.

29. This bon mot may have been coined by Sébastien-Roch Nicolas Chamfort; see Raunié, *Chansonnier historique,* vol. 1, p. i.

30. One box in the Bibliothèque de l'Arsenal, ms. 10319, contains dozens of these snippets, thrown together helter-skelter, which comment in rhyme on all sorts of current events—the amorous adventures of the regent, Law's fiscal system, the battles of the Jansenists and Jesuits, the tax reforms of the abbé Terray, the judicial reforms of the chancellor Maupeou—set to all kinds of popular tunes: "La Béquille du Père Barnabas," "Réveillez-vous belle endormie," "Allons cher coeur, point de rigueur," "J'avais pris femme laide." The repertory of melodies was inexhaustible, the occasions for drawing on it endless, thanks to the inventiveness of the Parisians and the rumor mill at work in the court.

31. BA, ms. 11683, fol. 59, report on the arrest of Mairobert by Joseph d'Hémery, July 2, 1749. The verse on the scrap of paper comes from a separate dossier labeled "*68 pièces paraphées.*" In a report to the police on July 1, 1749, a spy noted (fol. 55): "*Le sieur Mairobert a sur lui des vers contre le roi et contre Mme. de Pompadour. En raisonnant avec lui sur le risque que court l'auteur de pareils écrits, il répondit qu'il n'en courait aucun, qu'il ne s'agissait que d'en glisser dans la poche de quelqu'un dans un café ou au spectacle pour les*

répandre sans risque ou d'en laisser tomber des copies aux promenades . . . J'ai lieu de penser qu'il en a distribué bon nombre."

32. BA, ms. 11683, fol. 45.

33. Maurepas's love of songs and poems about current events is mentioned in many contemporary sources. See, for example, Rathery, *Journal et mémoires du marquis d'Argenson,* vol. 5, p. 446, and Edmond-Jean-François Barbier, *Chronique de la régence et du règne de Louis XV (1718–1765), ou Journal de Barbier, avocat au Parlement de Paris* (Paris, 1858), vol. 4, pp. 362–66.

34. Rathery, *Journal et mémoires de marquis d'Argenson,* 5: 448, 452, 456. The following version is taken from d'Argenson's account of this episode, 456. See also Barbier, *Chronique,* vol. 4, pp. 361–67; Charles Collé, *Journal et mémoires de Charles Collé* (Paris, 1868), vol. 1, p. 71; and François Joachim de Pierre, Cardinal de Bernis, *Mémoires et lettres de François-Joachim de Pierre, cardinal de Bernis (1715–1758)* (Paris, 1878), p. 120. A full and well-informed account of Maurepas's fall, which includes a version of the song that has "Pompadour" in place of "Iris," appears in a manuscript collection of songs in the Bibliothèque Historique de la Ville de Paris, ms. 649, pp. 121–27.

35. *Dictionnaire de l'Académie française* (Nîmes, 1778), vol. 1, p. 526: "*FLEURS, au pluriel, se dit pour* flueurs *et signifie les règles, les purgations des femmes . . . On appelle* fleurs blanches *une certaine maladie des femmes.*" Rather than a sexually transmitted disease like gonorrhea, this *maladie* might have been clorosis, or green-sickness.

36. In addition to the references given above, note 30, see Bernard Cottret and Monique Cottret, "Les Chansons du mal-aimé: Raison d'Etat et rumeur publique (1748–1750)," in *Histoire sociale, sensibilités collectives et mentalités: Mélanges Robert Mandrou* (Paris, 1985), pp. 303–15.

37. BA, ms. 11690, fol. 66.

38. I have discussed this affair at length in an essay, "Public Opinion and Communication Networks in Eighteenth-Century Paris," published in 2001 in a volume edited by Peter-Eckhard Knabe, *Opinion* (Berlin, 2000), pp. 149–230 and published separately as a book in German: Darnton, *Poesie und Polizei. Öffentliche Meinung und Kommunikatsions—netzwerke in Paris des 18. Jahrhunderts* (Frankfurt-am-Main, 2002). Its text, which contains references to a great deal of source material, can be consulted in the electronic version of this essay, on the *AHR* Web site, www.historycooperative.org/ahr. Most of the documentation comes from the dossiers grouped together in BA, ms. 11690.

39. Marc Pierre de Voyer de Paulmy, comte d'Argenson, to Nicolas René Berryer, June 26, 1749, BA, ms. 11690, fol. 42.

40. "Interrogatoire du sieur Bonis," July 4, 1749, BA, ms. 11690, fols. 46–47.

41. *Vie privée de Louis XV, ou principaux événements, particularités et anecdotes de son règne* (London, 1781), vol. 2, pp. 301–02. See also *Les fastes de Louis XV, de ses ministres, maîtresses, généraux et autres notables personnages de son règne* (Villefranche, 1782), vol. 1, pp. 333–40.

42. My own understanding of this field owes a great deal to conversations with Robert Merton and Elihu Katz. On Gabriel Tarde, see his dated but still stimulating work

L'Opinion et la foule (Paris, 1901) and Terry N. Clark, ed., *On Communication and Social Influence* (Chicago, 1969). For my part, I find Habermas's notion of the public sphere valid enough as a conceptual tool, but I think that some of his followers make the mistake of reifying it, so that it becomes an active agent in history, an actual force that produces actual effects, including, in some cases, the French Revolution. For some stimulating and sympathetic discussion of the Habermas thesis, see Craig Calhoun, ed., *Habermas and the Public Sphere* (Cambridge, Mass., 1992).

43. I have located and compared the texts of nine manuscript versions of this song. The first verse, quoted below and reproduced in Figure 10, comes from the scrap of paper taken from the pockets of Christophe Guyard during his interrogation in the Bastille: BA, ms. 11690, fols. 67–68. The other texts come from: BA, ms. 11683, fol. 134; ms. 11683, fol. 132; BNF, ms. fr. 12717, pp. 1–3; ms. 12718, p. 53; ms. 12719, p. 83; Bibliothèque Historique de la Ville de Paris, ms. 648, pp. 393–96; ms. 649, pp. 70–74; and ms. 580, pp. 248–49.

44. Albert B. Lord, *The Singer of Tales* (Cambridge, Mass., 1960), shows how the rhythms of poetry and music contribute to the extraordinary feats of memorizing epic poems.

45. Unfortunately, the *chansonnier* Maurepas stops in 1747, but the even richer *chansonnier* Clairambault extends through the mid-century years: BNF, mss. fr. 12717–20.

46. Bibliothèque Historique de la Ville de Paris, mss. 648–50.

47. P. Capelle, *La Clef du Caveau, à l'usage de tous les chansonniers français* (Paris, 1816) and J.-B. Christophe Ballard, *La Clef des chansonniers* (Paris, 1717). Most of the other "keys" are anonymous manuscripts available in the Fonds Weckerlin of the BNF. The most important for this research project are *Recueil d'anciens vaudevilles, romances, chansons galantes et grivoises, brunettes, airs tendres* (1729) and *Recueil de timbres de vaudevilles nottés de La Coquette sans le savoir et autres pièces à vaudeville* (n.d.). For help in locating this music, I should like to thank Hélène Delavault, Gérard Carreau, and Andrew Clark.

48. Louis Petit de Bachaumont, the doyen of Mme. Doublet's salon, had a lackey known as France: see Funck-Brentano, *Figaro et ses devanciers,* 264.

49. *Anecdotes sur Mme. la comtesse du Barry,* 167.

50. Ibid., 76.

51. Robert Darnton, *The Forbidden Best-Sellers of Pre-Revolutionary France* (New York, 1995).

52. Despite their official function, few *historiographes du roi* wrote contemporary history. The exception was Voltaire, whose *Siècle de Louis XV* reads like a political pamphlet in comparison with his magisterial *Siècle de Louis XIV.*

53. I have attempted to sketch the long-term history of *libelles* in *Forbidden Best-Sellers of Pre-Revolutionary France,* chap. 8.

Chapter 6 THE CRAZE FOR AMERICA

1. This account is based on a reading of the *Journal de Paris* from 1780 to 1789, along with other periodicals. The quotation about *Le Héro américain* comes from the issue of 17

June 1786. Beaumarchais referred to himself as *l'Américain* in a letter printed in the issue of February 13, 1785. The best of the many studies of French attitudes toward America are still Bernard Fäy, *L'Esprit révolutionnaire en France et aux États-Unis à la fin du XVIIIe siècle* (Paris, 1925) and Durand Echeverria, *Mirage in the West: A History of the French Image of American Society to 1815* (Princeton, 1957). In this essay I have drawn on my own thesis "The Gallo-American Society," submitted for the degree of Bachelor of Philosophy in the University of Oxford in 1962.

2. *Journal de Paris,* July 11, 1785. On Condorcet, the old biography by Léon Cahen, *Condorcet et la Révolution Française* (Paris, 1904) remains excellent and can be supplemented by the more recent one by Elisabeth and Robert Badinter, *Condorcet (1743–1794): Un intellectuel en politique* (Paris, 1988). The crucial work on Condorcet as a social scientist is Keith Baker, *Condorcet: From Natural Philosophy to Social Mathematics* (Chicago, 1975).

3. Condorcet, *Lettres d'un bourgeois de New-Haven à un citoyen de Virginie sur l'inutilité de partager le pouvoir législatif entre plusieurs corps,* in A. Condorcet O'Connor and François Arago, eds., *Oeuvres de Condorcet* (Paris, 1847–49), vol. 9, pp. 22–23 and 76.

4. Ibid., pp. 56 and 67.

5. See, for example, the "Anecdote sur les sauvages de l'Amérique Septentrionale" in *Journal de Paris,* March 12, 1785.

6. Condorcet, *De l'Influence de la révolution d'Amérique sur l'Europe* (1786), in O'Connor and Arago, *Oeuvres,* vol. 7, p. 28.

7. Ibid., pp. 16, 19, 27, and 37; quotations from pp. 28 and 37.

8. Jacques-Pierre Brissot, *Mémoires* (Paris, 1911) vol. 2, p. 48. The best biography of Crèvecoeur (whose name is usually anglicized as Saint John) is still J. P. Mitchell, *St. Jean de Crèvecoeur* (New York, 1916), and the best study of his writing remains H. C. Rice, *Le Cultivateur américain* (Paris, 1933).

9. Crèvecoeur, *Letters from an American Farmer* . . . (London, 1782), pp. 38–40, and *Lettres d'un cultivateur américain* . . . (Paris, 1784), vol. 1, pp. 171–76.

10. Fäy, *L'Esprit révolutionnaire en France,* pp. 50 and 136–37.

11. The expression comes from Georges Lefebvre, who entitled the chapter on 1790 in his great synthesis *La Révolution Française* (Paris, 1930) "L'Année de La Fayette." It does not imply that other revolutionaries, notably Mirabeau, were less important than Lafayette but rather that Lafayette occupied the center of the stage, at least for the period surrounding the Fête de la Fédération of July 14, 1790.

12. On the location of the bust and Mme. d'Enville's "parental affection" for Condorcet, see William Short to Thomas Jefferson, October 21, 1819, in the Jefferson Papers of the Massachussetts Historical Society. Quoted by Johanna Hecht in her essay in the present publication.

13. Brissot, *Mémoires,* vol. 2, p. 48.

14. Ibid., p. 49.

15. Ibid., p. 52.

16. Brissot, *Journal du Licée de Londres* (1784), vol. 2, p. 302.

17. Brissot, *Examen critique des voyages dans l'Amérique septentrionale de M. le marquis de Chastellux, ou lettre à M. le marquis de Chastellux, dans laquelle on réfute principalement ses opinions sur les quakers, sur les nègres, sur le peuple et sur l'homme* (London, 1786), p. 17. Brissot was seeing Crèvecoeur nearly every day by the end of June 1786: see Brissot, *Mémoires,* vol, 2, p. 49.

18. The minutes have been printed in Claude Perroud, ed., *J.-P. Brissot. Correspondance et papiers* (Paris, 1912), pp. 105–36.

19. Ibid., p. 109.

20. Brissot and Clavière, *De la France et des États-Unis, ou de l'importance de la révolution de l'Amérique pour le bonheur de la France, des rapports de ce royaume et des États-Unis, des avantages réciproques qu'ils peuvent retirer de leurs liaisons de commerce & enfin de la situation actuelle des États-Unis* (London, 1787), p. 130.

21. See, for example, ibid., pp. xxi and xxx–xxxi.

22. Crèvecoeur, *Lettres d'un cultivateur américain* (Paris, 1787), p. 3: letter 5.

23. Ibid., letter 10.

24. Excerpt from the *Mercure,* reprinted in Ibid. vol. 1, pp. xxiii–xxiv.

25. Brissot, *Examen.* Brissot wrote this diatribe of 143 pages after he was seeing Crèvecoeur virtually every day, but before the founding of the Gallo-American Society: see Brissot, *Mémoires,* vol. 2, pp. 46–47.

26. Brissot, *Examen,* vol. 2, p. 21.

27. Ibid., p. 121–22.

28. Brissot, *Mémoires,* vol. 2, p. 183. See also the similar remarks on p. 47.

29. Jean-François de La Harpe, *Correspondance littéraire, adressée à Son Altesse Impériale Mgr. le Grand-Duc, aujourd'hui Empereur de Russie* (Paris, 1801–1807), vol. 5, pp. 215–16.

30. Ibid., p. 216.

31. On Mazzei, a key figure in this story, see Raffaele Ciampini, ed., *Lettere di Filippo Mazzei alla corte di Polonia* (Bologna, 1937): Margherita Marchione, ed., *Philip Mazzei: Selected Writings and Correspondence* (Prato, Italy, 1983); and R C. Garlick, *Philip Mazzei. Friend of Jefferson: His Life and Letters* (Baltimore, 1933).

32. *Journal de Paris,* November 16 and 26, and December 5, 1786.

33. Filippo Mazzei, *Recherches historiques et politiques sur les États-Unis de l'Amérique septentrionale* (Paris, 1788) vol.4, pp. 140, 144, and 156, and Jefferson to John Adams, August 27, 1786, in *The Papers of Thomas Jefferson,* vol. 10, p. 302.

34. Mazzei to Madison, August 14, 1786, *Philip Mazzei: Selected Writings and Correspondence,* vol. 1, p. 530.

35. Le Mau de L'Ecossay to Jefferson, October 27, 1787, in *The Papers of Thomas Jefferson,* vol. 12, pp. 290–91.

36. Mazzei, *Recherches historiques,* vol. 4, p. 98.

37. *L'Analyse des papiers anglois,* vol. 2 (April 11, 1788), p. 368.

38. *Journal de Paris,* May 10, 1788. Although the letter did not carry Condorcet's name, it was signed "P.V.B.D.N.H.," which I take to be an acronym for *par un bourgeois de New Haven,* the *nom de plume* that Condorcet favored at that time. As far as I can determine, none of Condorcet's biographers have noticed this letter, nor have Jefferson scholars come across the pamphlet that he printed from Mazzei's *Recherches historiques.*

39. Léon Cahen, "La Société des Amis des Noirs et Condorcet," *La Révolution Française,* vol. 50 (1906), pp. 481–511, and Claude Perroud, "La Société Française des Amis des Noirs," ibid., vol. 69 (1916), pp. 122–47.

40. Condorcet expounded his analysis of the prerevolutionary crisis most cogently in his *Lettres d'un citoyen des Etats-Unis à un Français, sur les affaires présentes* (1788) and *Sentiments d'un républicain sur les assemblées provinciales et les Etats Généraux* (1789), both reprinted in O'Connor and Arago, *Oeuvres,* p. 9. On *la faction américaine du parlement de Paris,* see Joseph Weber, *Mémoires concernant Marie-Antoinette* (Paris, 1822), vol. 1, p. 180.

41. Mazzei reported on this conflict at some length in his correspondence with King Stanislaus Augustus Poniatowski of Poland. See especially his letter of November 21, 1788, in *Philip Mazzei: Selected Writings and Correspondence,* vol. 2, pp. 67–77, in which he noted this bit of dialogue: "Condorcet to me: 'If you go to M. de La Fayette's, try to exorcise the demon Aristocracy there to tempt him in the person of a Parlement counsellor or Breton nobleman. To do that, go carrying in your pocket a small vial of Potomac water and an aspergillum made from the stock of a Continental army rifle. . . .'"

42. *Eloge de Franklin,* in O'Connor and Arago, *Oeuvres,* vol. 3, pp. 407 and 420.

43. Of several references to the split between Condorcet and the d'Enville circle, the most vivid is a letter from Mazzei to King Stanislaus Augustus Poniatowski of December 22, 1791, in Marchione, *Philip Mazzei,* vol. 2, p. 678. In it he excoriated "that scoundrel, Brissot, the leader of the republicans, of whom Condorcet, who formerly considered him a mischief-maker or a raving madman, is now a follower rather than associate. His public behavior has finally prompted the Duchess d'Enville and the Duke de la Rochefoucauld to write two letters asking him to spare himself the trouble to call on them."

44. Jefferson to William Green Munford, Jr., February 27, 1799, transcript kindly supplied by John Catanzariti, editor of the Jefferson Papers in Firestone Library, Princeton University.

Chapter 7 THE PURSUIT OF PROFIT

1. The following account is condensed from a much longer study in my doctoral dissertation, *Trends in Radical Propaganda on the Eve of the French Revolution (1782–1788)* (Oxford, 1964). It owes a great deal to the work of Jean Bouchary, especially *Les*

Manieurs d'argent à Paris à la fin du XVIIIe siècle (Paris, 1939), 3 vols., and to J. Bénétruy, *L'Atelier de Mirabeau. Quatre proscrits genevois dans la tourmente révolutionnaire* (Geneva and Paris, 1962).

2. Mazzei's remark occurs in his *Memoirs*, tr. H. R. Marraro (New York), p. 229. I have tried to examine Brissot's financial difficulties and prerevolutionary career in "The Grub Street Style of Revolution: J.-P. Brissot, Police Spy," *The Journal of Modern History*, vol. 40 (1968), pp. 301–27. The best biography of him is still Eloise Ellery, *Brissot de Warville: A Study in the History of the French Revolution* (Boston, 1915).

3. Clavière's papers in the Archives Nationales include his "Copie de lettres," T*646 (1–3); his "Livre de caisse," T*646 (4); and his "journal," T*646 (5), as well as two cartons full of notes: T 646 (1) and T 646 (2). These documents are the main source for the following discussion of Clavière's finances and Brissot's pamphleteering. Clavière summarized his income from *rentes* in a journal entry dated April 1, 1786.

4. Papers of J.-C.-P. Lenoir, Bibliothèque municipale d'Orléans, ms. 1423, "Rapport de l'inspecteur ayant le département de la bourse."

5. Jacques-Pierre Brissot, *Mémoires de J.-P. Brissot (1754–1793), publiés avec étude critique et notes*, 2 vols., ed. Claude Perroud (Paris, 1911), vol. 1, p. 295.

6. I have transcribed all the entries in Clavière's papers that concern Brissot and have reconstructed Brissot's account with Clavière in *Trends in Radical Propaganda*, pp. 415–28, where a full version of the following excerpts may be read.

7. The best explanation of the techniques of speculating on the Bourse occurs in the pamphlets subsidized by Clavière, especially *De la Caisse d'escompte* (1785), published under the name of Mirabeau.

8. *Le Philadelphien à Genève, ou lettres d'un Américain sur la dernière révolution de Genève, sa constitution nouvelle, l'émigration en Irlande, etc., pouvant servir de tableau politique de Genève jusqu'en 1784* ("Dublin," 1783). As an example of Brissot's use of the *Social Contract* to justify his argument for popular sovereignty and the right of revolution, see pp. 66–67.

9. Clavière to the Société typographique de Neuchâtel, November 15, 1784, in the papers of the Société typographique, Bibliothèque publique et universitaire, Neuchâtel, ms. 1137.

10. Clavière to Brissot, April 10, 1783. At this time Brissot was planning to write a work on education for the colony that Clavière planned to found in Waterford, Ireland.

11. Brissot, *Mémoires*, vol. 2, pp. 28–29.

12. *Réponse de Jacques-Pierre Brissot à tous les libellistes qui ont attaqué et attaquent sa vie passée* (Paris, 1791), p. 22.

13. On Calonne's interest in the Compagnie des eaux, see Auget de Montyon, *Particularités et observations sur les ministres des finances de France les plus célèbres, depuis 1660 jusqu'en 1791* (London, 1812), pp. 255–56, and *Mémoires secrets pour servir à l'histoire de la république des lettres en France, depuis MDCCLXII jusqu'à nos jours* (London, 1784–1789), 36 vols., entry for November 14, 1787. The report of the baron de Batz is in *Gazette nationale, ou le Moniteur universel*, March 22, 1790.

14. *Sur les actions de la Compagnie des eaux de Paris* (London, 1785). On Clavière's speculation, see Bouchary, *Les Manieurs d'argent*, p. 63.

15. Pierre-Augustin Caron de Beaumarchais, *Réponse à l'ouvrage qui a pour titre: "Sur les actions de la Compagnie des eaux de Paris" par M. le comte de Mirabeau* (Paris, 1785), quotation from p. 11, and *Réponse du comte de Mirabeau à l'écrivain des administrateurs de la Compagnie des eaux de Paris* (Brussels, 1785), quotations from pp. 3 and 11.

16. Jacques-Pierre Brissot, *Dénonciation au public d'un nouveau projet d'agiotage, ou lettre à M. le comte de Sxxx sur un nouveau projet de compagnie d'assurance contre les incendies à Paris, sur ses inconvéniens, & en général sur les inconvénients des compagnies par actions* (London, 1786), quotations from pp. 33–35.

17. Jacques-Pierre Brissot, *Seconde lettre contre la Compagnie d'assurance pour les incendies* (London, 1786), quotation from p. 67. Clavière's letter to Casenove is quoted in Bouchary, *Les manieurs d'argent*, p. 71.

18. *Mémoires secrets*, entry for January 24, 1787.

19. See the minutes of the Society in Jacques-Pierre Brissot, *Correspondance et papiers, précédés d'un avertissement et d'une notice sur sa vie*, Claude Perroud, ed. (Paris, 1912), quotation from p. 132.

20. See the introduction by J. Bénétruy to Étienne Dumont, *Souvenirs sur Mirabeau et sur les deux premières assemblées législatives*, ed. J. Bénétruy (Paris, 1951), p. 14, and the rather vague remarks by Dumont himself, pp. 54 and 118, that provide the basis for Bénétruy's account in *L'Atelier de Mirabeau*, p. 131. In fact, Dumont did not arrive in Paris until August 1788 and had no firsthand experience of the financial pamphleteering of 1787. The most recent biographies of Mirabeau hardly mention the pamphleteering; see, for example, Guy Chaussinand-Nogaret, *Mirabeau* (Paris, 1982), p. 94. The older biographies provide some excellent accounts of it, but they did not draw on the information available in Clavière's papers; see Charles de Loménie, *Les Mirabeau, nouvelles études sur la société française au 18e siècle*, 4 vols. (Paris, 1889), vol. 3, p. 650, and Alfred Stern, *La Vie de Mirabeau par Alfred Stern, traduit de l'allemand par MM. Lespes, Pasquet & Pierre Péret*, 2 vols. (Paris, 1895), vol. 1, p. 272. For contemporary remarks linking Clavière to the *Dénonciation*, see Brissot, *Mémoires*, vol. 2, p. 29; A. M. de Cubières, *Mirabeau jugé par ses amis et par ses ennemis* (Paris, 1791), p. 91—"*C'est M. Clavière qui a fait presqu'en entier la* Dénonciation *de l'agiotage.* . . ."—and J.-P. Hardy, *Considérations sur la Dénonciation de l'agiotage. Lettre au comte de Mirabeau* (n.p., 1787), pp. 29–30. The bookseller S.-P. Hardy recorded in his journal on April 10, 1787, an extract from the *Correspondance littéraire secrète* that said Clavière had written part of the *Dénonciation*: Bibliothèque Nationale, mss. fonds français, 6687.

21. A. J. Gorsas, *Le Courrier des départements*, December 11, 1792.

22. *Dénonciation de l'agiotage au roi et à l'Assemblée des Notables. Par le comte de Mirabeau* (n.p., 1787), quotations from pp. 55 and 66–67.

23. For general discussions of d'Espagnac's coup and the Bourse crisis of 1787, see Marcel Marion, *Histoire financière de la France depuis 1715* (Paris, 1914); Herbert Lüthy, *La*

banque Protestante en France, de la révocation de l'Edit de Nantes à la Révolution, 2 vols. (Paris, 1961); Bouchary, *Les manieurs d'argent;* and George V. Taylor, "The Paris Bourse on the Eve of the French Revolution," *American Historical Review,* vol. 67 (1962), pp. 961–77.

24. The most thorough of the many accounts of Calonne and his program are Albert Goodwin, "Calonne, the Assembly of the French Notables of 1787 and the Origins of the 'Révolte Nobiliaire'," *English Historical Review,* vol. 61 (1946), pp. 202–34 and 329–77, and Jean Egret, *La Pré-révolution française (1787–1788)* (Paris, 1962), pp. 5–54. As an example of anti-Calonne views within the Notables, see Pierre Chevallier, ed., *Journal de l'Assemblée des Notables de 1787* (Paris, 1960). For a discussion of the pamphleteering against Calonne and reactions to it among readers, see my *Trends in Radical Propaganda,* pp. 234–69.

25. See the minutes of the society's meeting of March 27, 1787, in Brissot, *Correspondance et papiers,* pp. 131–33. The *Mémoires secrets* covered the Bourse conflicts extensively in articles that date from October 30, 1783, to November 14, 1787.

26. Bibliothèque Nationale, nouvelles acquisitions françaises, ms. 9534, fo. 410.

ACKNOWLEDGMENTS

THE CHAPTERS OF THIS BOOK WERE CONCEIVED AS PARTS OF A GENERAL ARGUMENT THAT EXTENDS FROM THE EARLY ENLIGHTENMENT TO THE FRENCH REVOLUTION, but they appeared as articles written at different times for different occasions. Some involve reports on research and therefore were published with full sets of references to sources and bibliography. Others are essays of a classical variety—that is, reflections on broad themes, which spill over from the eighteenth century into the present. Because the latter draw on general study rather than original research and are addressed to the general reader rather than to specialists, they do not include any scholarly apparatus. In the following acknowledgments, however, I should like to mention some of the secondary works that I found especially helpful. And I particularly want to acknowledge the help of two editors who have labored with me on these and many other texts: Robert Silvers of *The New York Review of Books* and Steven Forman of W. W. Norton & Company.

Chapter 1 was originally published as "George Washington's False Teeth" in *The New York Review of Books* (March 27, 1997), pp. 34–38.

Chapter 2 was originally given as the annual presidential address to the American Historical Association and appeared in modified form as "An Early Information Society: News and the Media in Eighteenth-Century Paris," *The American Historical Review,* vol. 105 (February 2000), pp. 1–35, and also as "Paris: The Early Internet" in *The New York Review of Books* (June 29, 2000), pp. 42–47. A much expanded version was published online at: www.indiana.edu/~ahr (now www.historycooperative.org/ahr). And a supplementary study of the circulation of poems and songs appeared as "Public Opinion and Communication Networks in Eighteenth-Century Paris," in Peter-Eckhard Knabe, ed., *Opinion* (Berlin, 2000), pp. 149–230.

Chapter 3 was written for a special issue of *Der Spiegel:* "Das Glück der Gemeinschaft," *Der Spiegel* (January 7, 2002), pp. 148–59. A somewhat different version appeared as "A Euro State of Mind," *The New York Review of Books* (February 28, 2002), pp. 30–32. Among many secondary works, it is indebted to Louis Réau, *L'Europe française au siècle des Lumières* (Paris, 1938) and Françoise Bléchet, ed., *Voltaire et l'Europe* (Paris, 1994).

Chapter 4 was adapted from a lecture given in Tokyo on October 6, 1993, to celebrate the opening of the Japanese Institute for Advanced Study and was published as "The Pursuit of Happiness" in the *Wilson Quarterly* (autumn 1995), pp. 42–52. A related essay, "What American Century?," appeared in *European Review,* vol. 7, no. 4 (1999), pp. 455–59. Both draw on a wide secondary literature, including: Robert Mauzi, *L'Idée du bonheur dans la littérature et la pensée françaises au XVIIIe siècle* (Paris, 1979); Howard Mumford Jones, *The Pursuit of Happiness* (Cambridge, Mass., 1953); Ursula M. von Eckardt, *The Pursuit of Happiness in the Democratic Creed* (New York, 1959); and Rhys Isaac, *The Transformation of Virginia 1740–1790* (Chapel Hill, 1982).

Chapter 5 originally appeared as "The Social Life of Rousseau: Anthropology and the Loss of Innocence" in *Harper's Magazine* (July

1985), pp. 69–73, and was reworked as "Rousseau in Gesellschaft," in Ernst Cassirer, Jean Starobinski, and Robert Darnton, *Drei Vorschläge Rousseau zu Lesen* (Frankfurt am Main, 1989), pp. 104–14.

Chapter 6 was published as "Condorcet and the Craze for America in France," in *Franklin and Condorcet: Two Portraits from the American Philosophical Society* (Philadelphia, 1997), pp. 27–39.

Chapter 7 was published as "Ideology on the Bourse," in Michel Vovelle, ed., *L'Image de la Révolution française* (Paris, 1989), vol. 1, pp. 124–39.

Chapter 8 was published as "How Historians Play God," in *Raritan: A Quarterly Review*, vol. 22, no. 1 (Summer 2002), pp. 1–19. It draws on a monograph that I published with the Voltaire Foundation as an electronic book: *J.-P. Brissot, His Career and Correspondence (1779–1787)* (Oxford, 2001): www.voltaire.ox.ac.uk.

INDEX

Page numbers in *italics* refer to illustrations.